Rakesh Anand is a trained Actor and Screenplay Writer from UCLA, Los Angeles, USA. After working in many Stage and TV/Video Productions in his hometown, Jammu, he decided to pursue his career in Hollywood... instead of Indian Film Industry. Well, everything was going fine with Anand's life in USA... but his faith in 'Astrology' just shattered his dreams!! After the expiry of his Student Visa, Anand should have stayed in USA but on his father's insistence and going by his Family-Astrologer's assurance that he would attain success during the 'Period of Mercury', Anand came back to India after filing for Immigrant Visa – even against the advice of his Immigration Attorney... but then, he could never go back to his Dream Land!!!

Utterly disappointed, Anand asked his 'Family-Astrologer' about his 'Hollywood Dream' many a time... but he never gave any 'justifying' answer. Anand then himself decided to know the 'Truth' about his 'Stars'!! He learned Astrology from a renowned Astrologer and began analyzing his horoscope as well as those of his nears and dears... and then he realized that there was something 'terribly wrong' with Astrology itself!! Shocked, he decided to do his own TESTING on Astrology to know the 'Truth'. He prepared horoscopes of 33 Test Subjects and obtained 101 Readings from Astrologers practising in different parts of India – his testing too proved that Astrology is merely a Superstition!!! Being a Writer himself, Anand then decided to write this Book so that the gullible people can get rid of this centuries-old extremely HARMFUL Superstition.

Though writing Books is an important step towards creating awareness... but Anand realizes fully well that a lot needs to be done since most people are only promoting Superstitions. In a bid to do so, Anand must set up an Anti-Superstition TV Channel 'HUMANITY' and create World's 1st Godless Commune of its own kind 'City of Humans' as envisioned in his Novel - 'Is God in Coma?' (aka, 'City of Humans')!!!

Astrology Tested FAKE

A research based book which proves that Stars and Planets do not affect the activities and events that occur in the life of an Individual

Rakesh Anand

DIAMOND BOOKS

www.diamondbook.in

Publisher : **Diamond Pocket Books (P) Ltd.**
X-30, Okhla Industrial Area, Phase-II
New Delhi-110020
Phone : 011-40712200
E-mail : sales@dpb.in
Website : www.diamondbook.in

Astrology Tested Fake
By: *Rakesh Anand*

Dedicated

to

the badly neglected

Cause

of

Eradication of

Fortune-Telling Superstitions

that still exist

in the

21st Century

Acknowledgement

This book would not have been possible if there were no internet. While learning astrology, when I realized that there was something wrong about it... that astrology did not provide any justifying conclusions... I wanted the answers... but did not find a single book that would question the validity of astrology - all the books on this subject just praised and taught astrology.

Very confused and dejected, I turned to my magic-box i.e. my internet connected laptop and started my new research at various search engines - what is wrong with astrology... why predictions go wrong... is astrology true... validity of astrology... is astrology scientific... and there I got the answers of these questions that inspired me to further conduct my own testing on astrology. After my testing convinced me that astrology does not work and that it is just one out of the many superstitions that still exist in the 21st century, I decided to write this book for awakening the innocent masses who are being exploited by the fortune-tellers.

I wholeheartedly appreciate the researchers and founders of the websites whose invaluable work has provided material for this book. The reference of such websites would be given in the respective pages.

I would specially like to thank founders of the website - www.wikipedia.org. This website is a good source of information on almost every subject.

The Agony

All the print and electronic media have a duty towards the society - to tell them the truth. But they prefer to show that 'truth' only which gets them more readership and viewership - in other words "more money". They are bothered only about their long term benefits even if it comes at the cost of misleading the society.

After writing the book, in the month of February 2008, I went to Delhi and informed the major national print and electronic media about my research. I was very excited and thought that with their help, the superstition of astrology would be vanished soon. But, to my great astonishment, not even a single so-called well wisher of the society showed any interest in my research. I proposed to them that their 'visiting' astrologers can take up my challenge - prove my research wrong and win an award of Rs.1,00,000/- but nobody listened. I came to know from some insiders in the media that the media was making huge profits from the business of astrology and that was the main reason that they didn't want any anti-astrology show! I was terribly disheartened and didn't know whom to contact for the fulfillment of my mission in Delhi. After wandering for some days in Delhi, I had no option but to go back home without any success.

But before packing my bags, I personally dropped copies of my book to the offices of - Mrs. Pratibha Devi Singh Patil (President of India), Dr. Manmohan Singh (Prime Minister of India), Mrs. Sonia Gandhi (President, Indian National Congress), Mr. Arjun Singh (Human Resource Development Minister), Mr. P. R. Das Munshi (Information and Broadcasting Minister) and Dr. Karan Singh (Member of Rajya

Sabha and former prince of pre-independence State of Jammu and Kashmir). Till date there is no response from anybody. One can well imagine that when the government and media of a country want to keep you in dark, no power on earth can help you. Well, in such circumstances, I truly miss being a celebrity myself. In that case, things would have been much easier - all the media would have been running after me for my interviews on my research. This would have been of great help in this mission.

The Resolve

But I have not yet lost the battle. I am sure that some intellectuals will come forward to help the innocent people get freedom from the misleading 'fortune-telling' systems. How long can we let some 50-100 bosses of media and those sitting in the power-chairs to misguide the society for their selfish motives? If I live for another 10-20 years, I would definitely root out this superstition.

Some Quotes about Astrology by the Author

Beware of astrologers - they are parasites on society.

★★★

Belief in astrology delays many marriages and in some cases destroys the life of those who really and most urgently need to get married but can not just because the horoscopes do not match (especially in India).

★★★

At 38 he lived a failed but (still) very carefree life as the astrologer had assured him that at the age of 40 when the period (*Mahadasha*) of Moon starts, riches will come. But by the age of 42, he was bankrupt and at the age of 45, he committed suicide because of financial crisis.

★★★

The astrologer predicted auspicious times ahead but it turned out to be the worst time of her life. Well, the astrologer had many reasons - the most common being that her time of birth was probably not correctly recorded.

★★★

Astrologers make hundreds of predictions in a day, some come true and they start boasting about their knowledge and advertise those predictions in the whole world.

★★★

Knowing all the means to please Star and Planet Gods, the astrologer himself lived a very miserable life and died a very pitiable death.

★★★

How amazing it is to see people still believe in astrology when they have already suffered a lot because of their faith!

Messages and Good Wishes

Many scholars of the past have criticized the practice of astrology and many more are still doing so...but astrology still exists! Here, comments about astrology in different religious scriptures and from prominent personalities of the past are being given first:

Mahatma Gandhi (Father of the Nation, India)
'I know nothing of the science of astrology and I consider it to be science, if it is a science, of doubtful value, to be severely left alone by those who have any faith in Providence.'

Voltaire (French Philosopher)
'Superstition is to religion what astrology is to astronomy: the mad daughter of a wise mother.'

Noel Coward (English Actor, Composer and Playwright)
'I don't believe in astrology. The only stars I can blame for my failures are those that walk about the stage.'

Robert Green Ingersoll (American Statesman and Orator)
'If the people were a little more ignorant, astrology would flourish - if a little more enlightened, religion would perish!'

Lawrence E. Jerome (Science Writer)
'How much physical and psychological damage such false astrological practices and advice cause, cannot even be estimated.'

Mahatma Buddha (Founder of Buddhism)
'Those that make a living by calculations of the Stars by such and other lying tricks are Parasites and must be avoided.'

Swami Vivekananda (Indian Scholar)
'I have seen some astrologers who predicted wonderful things; but I have no reason to believe they predicted them only from the stars, or anything of that sort. In many cases it is simply mind reading. Sometimes wonderful predictions are made, but in many cases it is arrant trash.'

Ibn Uthaymeen (Saudi Scholar)
'Astrology is kind of sorcery and fortune-telling. It is forbidden (in the Holy Quran) because it is based on illusions, not on concrete facts. There is no relation between the movements of celestial bodies and what takes place on the Earth.'

As per a quote from Bible
'Then came in the magicians, the astrologers, the Chaldeans, and the soothsayers: and I told the dream before them; but they did not make known unto me the interpretation thereof.'

As per a quote from Guru Granth Sahib
'You calculate the auspicious days, but you do not understand that the One Creator Lord is above these auspicious days... Do not tell lies, O pandit; O religious scholar, speak the Truth... Calculating and counting, the astrologer draws the horoscope. He studies it and announces it, but he does not understand reality.'

As per a quote from Quran
'He who uses astronomy for something other than what Almighty Allah has made lawful would be practising sorcery. Astrologists predict knowledge of the future, and he who does so is a sorcerer, and sorcerers are disbelievers.'

Well, after writing the book, the next step was to collect messages from some prominent personalities since people pay attention to what they say. It was an uphill task as most of the people (especially public figures) avoid involving themselves in the things that seem to them of controversial nature. So, after months of calling and waiting, most of them didn't respond (especially selfish and misleading media bosses). But, as they say, there is always a silver lining in the dark clouds - some of them decided to say something so that the innocent masses be benefited. I salute each one of them.

Shammi Kapoor (Indian Actor)
'I wish Rakesh all the best and hope that he succeeds in his efforts regarding this book.'

Suresh Dwadishwar (Editor, Lokmat Group of Newspapers, Maharashtra)
'Astrology has been surviving for a long time as it provides psychological comfort to the distressed people just because of their faith in it. But, with more people doing research and creating awareness through their works, such as this book 'Astrology Tested Fake', astrology may not survive for long.'

Waheeda Rahman (Indian Actress)
'It makes no sense to me to believe in astrology when it seems so full of confusing statements all the times - I wish Rakesh all the best in his mission.'

Dr. Sudhir Saxena (Editor, India News Magazine, New Delhi)
'Rakesh really deserves my heartily congratulations for his book entitled *'Astrology Tested Fake'*. We need such type of more and more books; this is the need of our time. I believe that one should have faith and confidence in themselves and follow the path of *karma*, as *karma* is the ultimate truth and nuclear factor.'

Manoj Kumar (Indian Actor, Director and Producer)
'Instead of running after astrologers and becoming a victim of superstitions, people should believe in *Karma-siddhant* (theory of performing one's duty) as advocated in *Bhagwat Gita.*'

Sharon Prabhakar (Indian Pop Singer)
'Astrology is one of the biggest superstitions of our times - just avoid it! The real mantra of success in life is - Do your best and believe in God.'

K. Srinivas (Editor, Andhra Jyothi Newspaper, Hyderabad)
'I fully appreciate Rakesh's efforts to counter unscientific tendencies in the society. Endeavors like this will go a long way in creating a future based on reason and reality.'

Tinu Anand (Indian Actor, Director and Producer)
'I believe that suggestions given by the astrologers don't really change anything - one should, therefore, have self-belief and work hard.'

Talat Aziz (Indian Ghazal Singer)
'Man's destiny is written by the Almighty and only He knows what the future holds - so, how can astrologers claim that they can predict the future? It's high time people should get rid of useless superstitions and learn to work hard.'

Bansi Lal Gupta (Editor, Early Times Newspaper, Jammu)
'Astrology is nothing but a superstition. One astrologer states one thing and the other something different. No star or planet can rule our life. I wish Rakesh all the best with his book and hope that this book would help innocent people get rid of this centuries-old superstition.'

Jaspal Bhatti (Indian Actor)
'This book seems to be good research work backed by 101 predictions (test readings of horoscopes of 33 test subjects) made by various astrologers - which were ultimately proved fake. I hope the authenticity of Rakesh's research gives him the power to fight fake astrologers.'

Bishambhar Newar (Editor, Chhapte Chhapte Newspaper, Kolkatta)
'The practice of astrology should not be encouraged but rather banned since the prediction side of astrology always misguides the masses and has no scientific basis.'

Jag Mohan Mundhra (Indian Writer, Producer and Director)
'I don't think that astrology has any rational explanation. Well, now astrologers should prove their point - this book openly challenges their science.'

Balraj Puri (Eminent Scholar and Political/Social Activist, J&K)
'Those who believe that reason has not conclusively proved that astrology is untrue, should accept the challenge of Rakesh Anand and win a handsome prize of Rs.10,00,000. If they have no courage to accept the challenge, they must gracefully fall in line with the contention of Rakesh Anand that astrology is a false science. In any case, I urge them to go through the well documented thesis of Anand with an open mind.'

Ved Rahi (Indian Writer and Director)
'I wish Rakesh all the best regarding his efforts to eradicate superstitions from our society. I myself have never believed in astrologers and always respect God's will.'

Ved Bhasin (Chairman, Kashmir Times Group of Publications, Jammu)
'The rising trend among the people in this country to believe in astrology, horoscopes, divine powers of the so-called godmen and miracles performed by them is a matter of grave concern as these go against scientific temper. These need to be exposed. It is in this context that the thorough study conducted by Rakesh Anand, author of '*Astrology Tested Fake*' will be highly appreciated. Such scientific pursuits, exposing astrology, myths and superstitions need to be commended. Astrology, which has not stood scientific scrutiny, cannot be accepted as a science and must be rejected by all rational human beings.'

Bhumicka Singh (Indian Actress)
'My congratulations to Rakesh for writing this book and I wish him a great success! I don't believe in astrology anymore. What I believe in is 5 D's i.e. Discipline, Dedication, Determination, Deadline and Destiny.'

Hasan Jawaid Khan (Editor, Science Reporter Magazine, New Delhi)
'Astrology has not stood the test of science time and time again, yet people look upon it as a handy crutch that will guide them through life. I have come across many people who have been influenced by this totally irrational belief in making some very unfortunate personal decisions. Although scientific tests proving astrology wrong abound in literature, it is commendable that Rakesh was driven to conduct his own tests. I hope his crusade succeeds in helping the people shed themselves of this irrational belief and they begin to think and plan their life for themselves.'

Prem Chopra (Indian Actor)
'This research-based book confirms my view that astrology does not work. May the un-aware masses be benefitted by Rakesh's research work!'

Dev Anand

(Evergreen Indian Actor, Writer, Producer and Director)

Success and failures are part of life - everybody goes through them. And I am not an exception. But I have never consulted fortunetellers during the long span of 87 years of my life. I have always believed in my own efforts and would keep on doing so.

I congratulate Rakesh Anand for writing this eye-opener book entitled *'Astrology Tested Fake'* and wish that this book sells very well so that Rakesh's message reaches the maximum number of people. I further assert that Rakesh be awarded for his revolutionary research work. It's high time that people learn to work hard, believe in their own efforts and get rid of misleading superstitions.

Khushwant Singh

(Internationally acclaimed Indian Journalist and Author)

I have always regarded futurology as a hoax, principally the widespread belief in astrology. Rakesh has researched the validity of astrology and found it without any foundation whatsoever. I recommend this book to be read by all Indians who still subscribe to this hoax, particularly men like Mr. Murli Manohar Joshi who introduced it as a subject in Indian universities.

(Mr. Singh has penned down many articles criticizing fortunetelling systems. Here's an excerpt from one of his articles published in Hindustan Times on May 2, 2008 - 'I would like to take a bet of any sum of money with believers in astrology: if they can as much as tell me what will happen to them and me the day following our wager and get it right, I will concede defeat and promise to keep my mouth shut ever after. However, if they can't foresee their own tomorrows, they must concede they cannot forecast what the future holds for others')

Baba Ramdev

(Internationally renowned Indian Yoga Teacher)

Vedas are divine knowledge and are purely scientific. There are four Vedas. The oldest scripture in the world is the *RigVeda*. In the Vedas, astrology (*Jyotish*) has been defined with respect to astronomical events such as Solar Eclipse, Lunar Eclipse, movement of Earth and other planets, etc. There is no mention in the Vedas which suggests that there is any effect of the movements of planets on humans and other living beings.

With the passage of time, many books based on false imagination were authored which misguided the gullible people to believe in futurology and hence their self-confidence was shattered - all this caused great loss to the society, nation and humanity. Till date, it has not been scientifically proved as to how the planets affect the activities and destiny of human beings.

Mr. Rakesh Anand, who is himself a creative and literary person, has tried to investigate the validity of astrology at an appropriate time.

I am pleased that after researching different aspects of astrology from different angles, he has come to this conclusion that the movements of planets don't have any direct relationship with the activities and destiny of human beings. This book entitled '*Astrology Tested Fake*' written on the basis of a lot of study, hard work and research, is a very praise worthy effort on the part of Mr. Rakesh Anand. I am very confident that this book would eradicate the preconceived notions regarding astrology, people would know the truth and would make progress in life by adhering to the principle of hard work - this all would lead to a strong society and nation. I wish that this book fully achieves its objective.

Aacharya Sukhdev Arya Tapasvi
(Renowned Veda Scholar/Orator)

As per God's principles, the Divine knowledge based on facts inspires one towards truth, peace, happiness, brotherhood, mercy, compassion and non-violence.

There is no mention of astrology (*phalit jyotish*) in any religion of the world and can never be. If there were any truth in astrology, there would not have been any poor, hungry or violent person. It all happens when one sins for one's own selfish motive. One who sins has discarded his/her religion. Religion only teaches and stresses on *karma* (doing one's duty).

Till date, nobody in the world has been able to predict as to where the stock piles of ammunition are concealed and where the terrorists are hiding. Had anybody predicted so, Delhi would not have been bombarded so many times!

In the present modern age, there is insincerity, untruthfulness, cheating and looting all around. I wish that in these circumstances, Rakesh's research-based book entitled '*Astrology Tested Fake*' guides human beings towards reality.

Vincent Concessao
(Archibshop of Delhi)

I would like to congratulate Mr. Rakesh Anand who has thoroughly studied astrology by collecting data from various astrologers and shown that astrology has no scientific basis and that the claims of many an astrologer are fake. It is important that we do not encourage superstitions based on ignorance when matters are objects of scientific investigation. It is important that we make use of the tools we have to ensure that we get to the truth of the reality around us. To make real progress we need to build on truth.

I am sure that the study of Mr. Rakesh Anand will contribute towards this objective.

Krishan Kumar Suman

(Chief Editor, Yog Manjri - Magazine dedicated to Yoga)

In this scientific age, one should not depend on astrology (*phalit jyotish*) which is based on probabilities and speculations. The astrologers, through their tricky and double-meaning speculative language, exploit the gullible, ambitious and hapless people who want to mitigate their present sufferings and are curious to know about the future events of their life. The astrologers fully exploit these people while making them even more restless and dissatisfied.

Generally, the people with low self-confidence are more curious to know about their future. They believe in providence. The people who are very ambitious and those left with no hope often get attracted towards the astrologers and occultists who exploit them by making false promises.

I myself had keen interest in astrology and have studied numerous books on the subject. I got horoscopes of my family members cast from many astrologers but there was neither any similarity in predictions nor did they come true.

It is a matter of great appreciation and courage on the part of Mr. Rakesh Anand that he has taken up this challenging task to eradicate the superstition of astrology. This book would help millions of people in removing their misconceptions and ignorance about the truth of astrology.

Alhaj Mohd. Amin Khan

(Principal, Madrasa Ashraf-ul-Aloom, Jammu)

Astrology is like other baseless beliefs adopted by the man, which are superstitions and illusions and in no way helpful and beneficial for the human beings.

As per our Islam religion: we should completely surrender before the Almighty *Allah* who is supreme. Man is next to *Allah* and superior to everything else such as Sun, Moon, Stars, etc. They work for us like our servants. They are not important for us. We should obey the order of *Allah* and should not have fear of anything else.

Rakesh deserves my heartily congratulations for taking up the task of writing such an educating book, especially in the times when media is hell bent upon misguiding the innocent people. I pray to *Allah* to grant Rakesh success in his endeavors.

Dr. Prem Dutt Pandey

(Chief Editor, Nirogadham - Magazine dedicated to Ayurveda)

After reading the manuscript of '*Astrology Tested Fake*', I am surprised and impressed to see Rakesh's undying spirit in trying to understand the truth and usefulness of astrology. I whole heartedly appreciate Rakesh's mission, the hard work he is doing for the completion of his mission and the way he is handling this subject with complete sincerity, devotion and honesty.

I myself have done a great deal of study in astrology from 1960 to 1970, learned its calculative part, practised the art (not science any more) by casting hundreds of horoscopes free of cost but finally I also came to the conclusion that the calculative part (*ganit jyotish* i.e. astronomical part) of astrology was alright but there was no scientific justification and truth in its predictive part (*phalit jyotish* - astrological part). After realizing this unbelievable truth (at that time), I gave up the practice of astrology because predictive part of astrology is based only on misconceptions, probabilities and speculations.

I wish that Rakesh succeeds in his efforts and achieves his revolutionary objective to remove widespread misconceptions regarding astrology prevailing in the whole world.

Lobsang Dhamchoe

(Secretary, Ladakh Budhist Vihara, New Delhi)

I am very pleased that Rakesh has been working hard for the last many years in order to bring awareness among the people around this world to eradicate these misleading superstitions. I know that this noble action in order to educate the people would be very difficult and I could see the road ahead to be very challenging for Rakesh and his team when astrology has become very popular these days.

As a Budhist monk and follower of *Lord Buddha*, I learn that my Lord had always taught his followers about the practical aspect of life and the same must be by the founders of other religions.

Those who try to gain the attention of ignorant people, using an act of predicting in life in order to earn and gain from the same, are not the enlightened ones but are a bunch of cunning parasites and will never get success in life by themselves.

I congratulate Rakesh and his team for their bold act to educate the innocent masses. I always teach others that the fruit you get is the outcome of your actions (*karma*). Rakesh's endeavor to enlighten and liberate the masses from the hands of such misleading astrologers is highly appreciable. My best wishes and support be always with Rakesh for his good work.

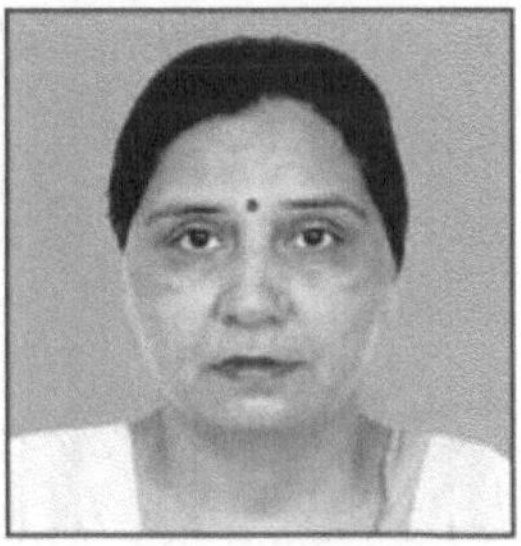

Sulekha Palaha

(Editor, Vaidya Raj - Magazine dedicated to Ayurveda)

Rakesh deserves my heartily appreciation for undertaking this brave effort and writing *'Astrology Tested Fake'*. In today's world, astrologers and occultists exploit the superstitious psyche of the masses and practise astrology as a means for making money. The remedies as suggested by the astrologers have no mention in the *Shastras* (Hindu religious scriptures) but because of the superstitious psyche of the gullible people, astrology has flourished as a very profitable business.

Rakesh is sure to face a lot of criticism because of his efforts, though he is working for a noble cause. I pray to God that Rakesh gets success in his mission.

Vaidya Raj group's warmest wishes are with him for the success of this book!

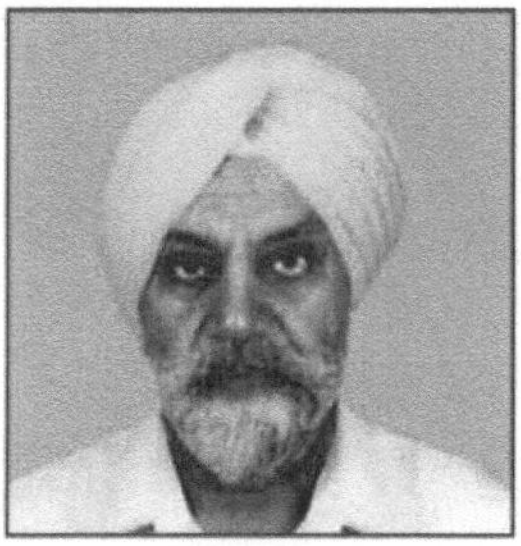

Dalip Singh

(President, Distt. Gurudwara Prabandhak Committee, Jammu)

Astrology contrary to other social sciences has no fixed/set principles or universal dogmas. It is as such a mere superstition/ illusion which weakens the will power and determination. Even the persons who are not adequately educated boast to be astrologer/ fortunetellers and exploit the masses. Had it been possible to foresee the future, there would have been no misery/pain to anybody; at least the astrologer could have saved himself and his family from the eventuality.

As per Sikh religion, man's destiny is governed by his '*karma*' (deeds).

"As you sow so shall you reap"

True faith in Almighty, righteous deeds, determination and dedication are the real guide of man's destiny. Auspicious/ inauspicious is all will of "*Creator*", the God.

To dispel the superstition of astrology, "*Astrology Tested Fake*" is an effort in the right direction. I wish Rakesh success in his efforts.

Almighty's choicest Blessings!

Kailash Yogiraj

[Temple Head (*Mahant*), Ati Praachin Shiv Mandir, Jammu
Swamiji is renowned for 21-day 'under-ground' Samadhi]

Not only in India but all over the world, ancient scholars and researchers studied the positions and movements of Stars and Planets roaming about in the sky. Due to prevalent religious beliefs of their times, many of them thought the astronomical bodies to be Gods and believed that these Gods influence the destiny of earth and human beings. With the passage of time, these ignorant researchers added more and more superstitions to their 'knowledge of stars'. Nonetheless, their research enlightened ancient human beings about the knowledge of - directions, timings of different seasons, solar and lunar eclipses, etc.

Well, from time to time, many renowned scholars have condemned the practice of astrology and advised the masses not to indulge in it. But to the worst disappointment of our times, astrology is becoming even more popular due to the influence of print and electronic media. One can find advertisements of astrologers and astrological goods everywhere - Newspapers, Magazines, Books, T.V. Channels, Internet, etc. The point is very clear - Astrology is a multi-billion dollar business. The people dealing in the business of astrology spend millions on print and electronic media advertisements and then earn billions in return. So, in this way, astrologers and media are a good choice for each other. In the present age of tension and worries, there is no dearth of people who would like to try out any 'supernatural remedy'.

Now, at a time, when print and electronic media is so selfish and influential, I doubt whether they would even pay attention to Rakesh's research. But, through this message, I would very humbly request them to realize their duty and stop misguiding the innocent people.

Lastly, I wholeheartedly appreciate Rakesh's research work and wish that '*Astrology Tested Fake*' will educate the ignorant masses of the world. I further assure him that we all are with him in this noble mission of eradicating the superstition of astrology.

CONTENTS

INTRODUCTION

First of all, I would like to congratulate you for your interest in this book. I am hundred percent confident that after reading this book, you would definitely get rid of useless and misleading fortune-telling superstitions, learn to work hard, believe in your own efforts and enjoy a fearless life. I would be most delighted and rewarded when I get your 'confession' cum 'transformation' letters.

Well, the title of this book clearly suggests that astrology (the system that generally uses 'horoscopes' for divination purposes) has been tested fake – and though my research and testing have proved that astrology is fake but here I would like to make it clear that I am pointing towards other fortune-telling systems also that often claim 'effects' of Stars and Planets on human beings such as numerology and palmistry. Moreover, I disapprove of all other systems that claim divination through different means such as tarot cards, crystal balls, ritual calendars, divine animals, etc – the list of such non-sensical superstitions is endless. What I am trying to convey to you is that after reading this book, when you stop visiting 'astrologers' – don't start running after other 'fortune-tellers'... please! All fortune-telling systems are baseless superstitions of ancient humans, well, though there are still many superstitious people in the 21st century – I would request you not to be one of them.

Most people go to astrologers at some point of time in their life whether they confess it or not, or they like it or not. Either they are in some problem and want some super-natural intervention to solve their problem or they are just curious about their future and want to correct bad effects of malefic stars in advance.

My life has been full of many diverse experiences for the last 20 years. My mother's un-timely death in my teens turned my attention towards religion, spiritualism and astrology. At the age of 18, I had read *'Autobiography of a Yogi'* by Paramhans Yogananda. In one of the chapters of the book, Yoganada's *guru* (Teacher) Sri Yukteshwar had advocated astrology, though initially Yogananda was reluctant to believe in astrology, but later Yogananda had accepted it. Since I was very much influenced by Yogananda and felt myself to be a *Yogi* like him, I too accepted astrology. I was confident that by following instructions of the astrologers, bad effects of malefic stars in my horoscope will be mitigated and I would attain success. As time progressed, besides putting my best efforts, I showed my horoscope to many astrologers in Jammu, Delhi, Haridwar, Rishikesh, Jodhpur, Bombay, Los Angeles, San Diego, etc. - wherever I went and followed their instructions. Some predicted my career in our family business, some in music and some in films, some predicted my success in India and some in USA and so on.

Most of the predictions failed the test of time but still I had no problem with astrology until three years back when I decided to learn astrology for the sake of my personal interest. I learned to cast horoscope manually from a professional astrologer and it took me about six months to be able to cast horoscopes for myself, my wife and my father. One day my astrology teacher suggested me to do 'astrology business' on partnership basis with him. He knew astrology well and I had a place, an internet-connected computer and the money for promoting the business through Press, TV and most importantly, Internet advertising. I really liked the idea but, due to some personal reasons, agreed to start the business of astrology at some later stage. Well, in the meantime, I started reading books on the prediction part of astrology and started analyzing my own horoscope. I matched formulae given in different books that applied to my horoscope and tried to figure out the outcome but miserably failed to understand what the 'Planet and Star Gods' actually conveyed. As per one formula, my life seemed very good and as per the other very bad. In addition, there seemed not a few probabilities but the probabilities reflected by various formulae seemed endless. I was confused and consulted my astrology teacher. The teacher revealed that there were many factors for contradictory results but I, somehow, was not very satisfied by his explanations. Well, still having no doubt in astrology, I kept doing my study of astrology.

Here's one of the most interesting incidents of my life regarding my faith in astrology: After my wife got pregnant, she always told me that she would not go for 'normal delivery' but would opt for cesarean surgery. So, when the time came on 6th of August, 2006, I admitted her into a nursing home. Then, out of curiosity, I began to consult *panchang* (ephemeris) to know the positioning of *Star and Planet Gods*. But soon, I was horrified to know that on that day, *gandmool nakshatra* was to remain until 11-15 PM [A child born during *gandmool nakshatra* is said to bring inauspicious times not only for him/her self but for other members of the family also (even death of father), etc. Moreover, father is not expected to see the child for 27 days and on the 27th day, certain *poojas* (ceremonial worship) have to be performed]. So, what do I do now? Immediately, a superb idea flashed through my mind and I started complimenting myself for my astrological knowledge. I instructed the doctor to perform the surgery any time after 11-15 PM. Now, my wife, who had been suffering from severe labor pains, started abusing and cursing my decision. But, I would not listen. What was the use of my astrological knowledge if I did not make use of it in time? So, ultimately, my daughter, Moksha, was born at 11-27 PM. (I had already decided her name as the word *Moksha* has very philosophical meaning – it means freedom from the repeating cycle of 'birth and death'). Immediately, after Moksha's birth, I prepared her natal chart. All my relatives were astonished to know about my newly attained knowledge. Quite excited, I boasted in front of all of them that my name should be registered in the Guinness Book of World Records for 'having cast the natal chart of a person instantly after his/her birth'. Everybody praised me and started requesting that I prepare their horoscopes too. I must say that I really felt very honoured and proud at that moment!

Well, after some weeks of Moksha's birth, I consulted my astrology teacher regarding Moksha's future and was given some instructions. A few days later, I consulted another astrologer friend of mine and noted down his instructions also. Moreover, after studying some books on predictive astrology, I noted down various instructions and predictions as per Moksha's horoscope. But again, the same problem arose – I could not get to any conclusion. Those were the days when I started sensing that there was something wrong with astrology. But, still I didn't lose faith in astrology.

Actually, the reason for my utmost faith in astrology was due to the following reasons:

1. Some astrologers had accurately read some of the past and present events of my life
2. Paramhansa Yogananda had advocated astrology in his autobiography
3. All my family and the world seemed to believe in astrology

But then, after some research, I came to know that the few astrologers, who had read my past correctly, were famous for having attained some kind of '*siddhis*' (ability to contact super-natural powers/ higher spirit forms or developed some sort of psychic/clairvoyant abilities). Those *siddhis* can reveal your past and present situation and are believed to give some guidance about the future but the guidance/ predictions regarding future can't be taken seriously at all (well, if you are sure that there is no such power as *siddhi* and that I am misguided, kindly guide me). Even I myself used to invoke Spirits and take guidance from them when I was about 20 but, in my experience, all that Spirits revealed about past, present or future was useless. So, after a couple of months I had left the practice once and for all.

Well, it now started coming to my mind as to why there were so many probabilities in astrology and why the things don't match. Why only the astrologers with the power of '*siddhi*' could tell something correctly about the past and not all astrologers? And, why even the astrologers with the power of '*siddhi*' could not correctly predict about the future? Is there something wrong with the astrologers or, something wrong with astrology itself?

With these doubts in mind, I decided to conduct research on the validity of astrology. Now, I became so impatient to know the truth that I decided to rent out my restaurant for a period of one year so that I could devote my full time and concentration to my research. I also rejected/postponed all my television contracts that I sometimes get as an actor, writer and producer. Well, after renting out my restaurant, I changed the job duties of my restaurant manager, Mukesh. He was now my assistant in my research work and has been of some help in this project. Having all the things arranged, I started my new study i.e. research about the validity of astrology. First of all, I wanted to read some books on the topic but, surprisingly, could not find a single book questioning the validity of astrology! Of course, there are hundreds of books which teach astrology. Disappointed, I turned to my magic box i.e. my internet-connected laptop, which has always given me valuable information when I needed it the most (without any contact in USA and without the help of an agent, it was through my magic box that I got admission in UCLA, Los Angeles, USA where I successfully completed a two-year Screenwriting program).

So, after browsing on the internet for months together, I came up with the startling revelation that astrology is fake. Many western scientists and researchers had conducted detailed research and testing on astrology and found it to be fake.

Now, I got the clue from there to conduct my own research and testing on astrology. I collected birth information of many famous/infamous personalities (Indian as well as International) from internet and astrological magazines but chose only 24 as my test subjects and cast their horoscopes. Also, I collected horoscopes of 9 people I knew personally. So, overall I had 33 horoscopes to test the validity of astrology myself. I started my mission from my hometown, Jammu and then covered Jalandhar, Ludhiana, Kurukshetra, Delhi, Mathura and Gokul. I showed these horoscopes to astrologers of all kinds - the ones who had inherited the gift of astrology from their ancestors, those who had been practising astrology for the last 50 years, those who also claimed many super-natural powers and those who had completed some sort of diploma/degree in astrology - those who had fixed their consultation fee to not less than 1000 rupees and those who accepted whatever amount is offered to them. Ultimately, I obtained 101 readings for these 33 horoscopes.

But, to my great disappointment, no astrologer could correctly read the past events occurred in the life of my test subjects. Just imagine this: You show the horoscope of George Bush (changing the name) and the astrologer tells that there was/is no political career for this person or you show the horoscope of Amitabh Bachchan (changing the name) and the astrologer tells that there was/is no art career for this person or you show the horoscope of Bill Gates and the astrologer tells that there was/is no big money for this person and... this happens with all the horoscopes you show. What would you think? If the horoscopes can't reveal your past, what can they reveal about your future? The obvious point is that astrology is a misleading and a useless superstition.

Whatsoever, astrology has been a very fascinating subject for millions of people all around the world. It has a unique appeal and unparalleled capacity to misguide almost everybody on planet Earth! Moreover, it provides hope to many people at the same time. So, in a way, I do have a lot of respect for the ancient astrologers because they worked so hard, whatsoever, to discover 'astrology'. But, it's also true and need of the time that we can't afford to live in "imaginary worlds" anymore. It harms everybody and it has harmed me a lot too. That's what has prompted me to write this book so that innocent people be not harmed anymore.

I hope you enjoy reading this book as much as I have enjoyed writing this.

ASTROLOGY: A BRIEF OVERVIEW

The word astrology is derived from the Greek words ἄστρον - astron, meaning "constellation, star", and λογία - logia, meaning "the study of" - that generally means study of relative positions and movements of the Stars and Planets in order to understand their influence in the life of a subject (an individual, a nation, a business, etc.). Astrologically, the sky has been divided into twelve constellations (groups of stars that seem to form imaginary distinctive shapes) commonly known as Twelve Signs of the zodiac. Observing the positioning of different planets in relation to the constellations at the time of birth of a subject, an astrologer casts a horoscope. The astrologers claim that a horoscope can reveal all the events - past, present and future - in the life of a subject and offer solutions for removing unwanted effects of Stars and Planets.

Well, it has been observed that any person (astrologer, palmist, numerologist, tarot card reader, clairvoyant, etc.) who is believed to interpret past, present or future events in the life of a subject is commonly misunderstood by the masses (especially Indians) as an astrologer. Moreover, many people even mistake astrology for astronomy. Astronomy deals with the scientific study of the physical properties, origin, development, positions and movements, effects, etc. of the astronomical bodies whereas astrology is concerned with the study of favourable and unfavourable decree of Star and Planet Gods (or angels of God or Demi-Gods, whatsoever) regarding a subject. The difference between the two can be very easily understood by the following example: Both astronomy and astrology study and recognize the relationship between the Moon and the oceanic tides but astrology would go further and describe the good and bad effects of Moon for different human beings (as per their horoscopes) as if Moon is choosing the favourites among the billions for rewards while punishing others. In this way, Moon is like a God or an instrument of God through which God rewards or punishes Earth and its inhabitants.

From this point of view, astrology is more like a religion where all the Stars and Planets are some *sort of Gods* or *angels of God* that control all the events on the Earth and in the life of its inhabitants.

In those times when astrology was being formulated, apart from worshipping the *Gods of the Sky*, ancient humans worshipped many other Gods such as the *River God, Tree God, Rain God, Mountain God, Snake God, Earth God, etc.* Interestingly, astrology is also accepted by many a people whose religious beliefs suggest only One God such as Jews, Christians and Muslims. Well, it could be understood as a result of the influence of old nature religions that were pre-existing before the advent of these religions. Also, it could be due to the influence of the followers of other religions such as Hinduism.

The history of astrology goes back to the time when the primitive humans started living in societies and developed their respective mythological stories about the creation of universe and life on earth. So, one would find that almost all the civilizations had their own mythological beliefs while worshipping numerous Gods - Indians believed *Brahma* and *Vishnu* to be the Creators of universe, Babylonians considered *Aapsu, Tiyamat* and *Marduk* responsible for Creation, Egyptians worshipped God Rey as the Creator, Greeks considered *Jeyus* as the Creator of humans, Japanese worshipped *Izanami* and *Izanagi* as the Creators of universe, etc. Similarly, all other civilizations had their own respective Gods whom they worshipped as the Creator of the universe. Later on, many religions originated from these mythological beliefs claiming only themselves to be true and others fake. From the point of view of an analytical mind, all seem fake. A child cannot have 100 fathers!

Living on a flat Earth and considering it to be the centre of the universe, the primitive humans had learnt a lot about the power of their mythological Gods - How the *Sky Gods* (Sun, Moon, Stars and Planets) sometimes brought pleasant sunshine while sometimes windstorms, sometimes brightened the sky in the night and sometimes just disappeared keeping them in darkness, sometimes showered rains for the better production of vegetation and sometimes for their destruction ... How the *Earth God* that gave them shelter and food, sometimes caused earthquakes ... How the *River God* that provided them water, sometimes caused floods, etc. etc. - this all led them to fear and worship these Gods and this happened almost everywhere.

Gradually, they learned to keep track of the *Sky Gods* in order to understand their message. With the development of calendar systems, it became easier to keep record of the days, months and years. Now, if something good happened at a specific time on a specific day and in the next cycle on the same time and day, if something good happened again, it convinced them that the *Sky Gods* of that moment were 'auspicious'. Similarly, 'inauspicious', 'very inauspicious', 'less-auspicious', 'highly-auspicious' Gods were imagined along with combination of other Gods. It was a very laborious and time consuming task and special priests were appointed to do this job. In the beginning, astrology was being used for the Kings and the State but thereafter, it became popular with the masses.

Now, as the humans started living together in civilizations, their belief systems got exchanged with one another - further giving birth to more complex belief systems and astrological formulae. And, as the civilizations interacted with one another, the belief systems grew like mushrooms. Many more astrological formulae for deriving 'auspicious' as well as 'inauspicious' times were formulated.

Later, with the passage of time, belief systems of many civilizations witnessed dramatic transformations due to certain political and religious impacts but still astrology is practised the world over.

TRADITIONS OF ASTROLOGY

Honestly, I have no intention to write a big fat 'anti-astrology' book but I think that it would be interesting to know a bit about the history and traditions of astrology. How astrology was developed in different parts of the world? How so many formulae and theories were formulated? How different cultures while interacting with one another, exchanged and adopted astrological principles? Though, many of the questions will always remain un-answered but we can still have some good idea about the whole thing. And most importantly, we should not be very concerned about the accuracy of whatsoever is written about the history of astrology in different cultures because there can never be a specific way to ascertain the accuracy of history of that period. There have always been many historians, researchers, scholars and authors throughout the history of humankind but the actual facts seldom remain the same as the time passes by, especially in times when people didn't know about writing. Oral stories passed from one generation to the other, there was no system of maintaining records and no printing press. Every author would add new things as per their own faith and liking. French would write that France was superpower in so and so year and (given a chance) the German would amend and write that Germany was the superpower. So, we should not get into a debate whether astrology started from India or Mesopotamia or Egypt unless we have free time in hand and want to waste it somehow.

Well, I would like to mention it here that many so-called scholars often argue with me that astrology started from India and thereafter spread in the whole world... they ask me many typical questions about the history of astrology in India... test my knowledge about astrologers who lived in different parts of India and wrote fabulous books on astrology, and things like that. Now, when I tell them that I don't need to know much about Indian astrologers or Indian Astrology, they get irritated and taunt that 'astrology' is not fake but '*Astrology Tested Fake*' is fake. It amuses me. Now, I counter question them and test their knowledge of astrology in other parts of the world. They just don't seem to be in any mood of discussing that and simply declare that originally astrology started from India and then spread to the whole world and that other systems are fake. It amuses me even more.

Well, the point here is that we should not be concerned about the history of astrology or astrologers but with the validity of astrology. And the truth is that astrology is just a superstition and that has been proved not only by me but by many researchers the world over. And that's what this book is all about.

Now, let's get a general perspective of some of the most known astrological systems of the world without going into their detailed history.

Mesopotamian Astrology
Egyptian Astrology
Hellenistic Astrology
Arabian/Persian Astrology
Western Astrology
Indian Astrology
Chinese Astrology
Meso American Astrology

MESOPOTAMIAN ASTROLOGY

The origin and development of the twelve constellations (Sun Signs of the Western and *Rashis* of the Indian Astrology) is believed to have taken place in the Mesopotamian region (better known for Babylonian civilizations. Mesopotamia was a region around the Tigris and Euphrates rivers, which now falls in some parts of Turkey, Syria and Iraq). Just like other civilizations, the Mesopotamian civilizations also worshipped many Gods of Creation and some of those Gods were associated with different Signs and Planets. *Apsu* and *Tiamat* were believed to be the first Gods of Creation and *Marduk* was believed to be the Creator of human beings.

Large and high structures called '*Ziggurats*' (some of them as high as 300 feet) were built to study the positions of the favourable and unfavourable Planet and Star Gods. Initially, the Babylonian astrologers plotted eighteen constellations but later on by 300 BCE, only twelve constellations of the zodiac were fixed. Following is the list of different Constellations and Planets of the Babylonian era:

Constellations:

1. Luhunga (Aries)
2. Guanna (Taurus)
3. Mash (Gemini)
4. Nangar (Cancer)
5. Ura (Leo)
6. Absin (Virgo)
7. Zihanitum (Libra)
8. Girtab (Scorpio)
9. Pah (Sagittarius)
10. Suhur (Capricorn)
11. Gula (Aquarius)
12. Zib (Pisces)

Planets:

1. Shamas (Sun)
2. Sin (Moon)
3. Ishtar (Venus)
4. Nebo (Mercury)
5. Nergal (Mars)
6. Ninurta (Saturn)
7. Marduk (Jupiter)

The Babylonian astrologers and mathematicians have contributed a lot to astrology and modern astronomy; they succeeded in creating an accurate calendar, identified the cycles of Sun and Moon, divided the year into 12 months, divided a day into 24 hours, each hour into 60 minutes and each minute into 60 seconds. These ancient units of time are still in use.

As of 1996, only sixteen Babylonian horoscopes have been found but they contain hardly any prediction. They mostly consist of the position of the skies at the time of birth of the individual.

EGYPTIAN ASTROLOGY

Egypt (best known for its mummies and pyramids) is also considered as an important centre for the development of astrology. The Egyptians were deeply religious and their most notable religious belief was in 'life after death'. They worshipped many Gods and some of them were attributed to Planets and Stars. The supreme God of Egyptian religion was *Re* - the Sun God, who produced *Shu* - God of Air and *Tefnut* - Goddess of Moisture. Now, this couple produced *Geb* - the Earth God and *Nut* - the Sky Goddess and so followed the Creation.

The Egyptians had great respect for *Re* and *Sirius* - the Dog God as they believed that the combined action of them both brings floods in the Nile River which was instrumental to their survival because without floods their lands would have remained a barren desert. The Egyptian Kings known as *Pharaohs* had a great interest in astrology due to their religious faiths. Rameses II, who ruled Egypt sometime between 1200 - 1085 BCE, had a remarkable sky map carved on his tomb. It was possible to read from this map the culmination of Stars for each hour of the night throughout the year. Some Star charts have been found in Egypt that date back as far as 4200 BCE.

Egyptian astrologers are believed to have developed some of the Signs of the zodiac such as Aries, Gemini, Leo and Virgo. *Cairo Calendar* is also a good source of information about the Egyptian astrology. The Egyptians arranged 365 days of the year into 36 weeks of 10 days each which were called '*decades*'. In Egyptian astrology, great importance has been given to these '*decades*' which represented certain Gods or Demons who exerted their influence when Sun passed through them.

One of the most notable features of Egyptian astrology is that it developed a unique system of medicine called '*Iatromathematics*'. They designated different Planet and Star Gods for different Stones, Animals, Human organs, Plants, etc. In case of an illness, designated God of that particular affected part/organ of the body would be recognized and then accordingly, Stones, Plants or Animal products corresponding to the designated God would be used to heal that organ. Similar sort of practice can be seen in India even today.

HELLENISTIC ASTROLOGY

The Greek king Alexander conquered the large parts of the Mediterranean region and central Asia in the 4th century BCE and united them into one empire. In 331 BCE, he founded the city of Alexandria in Egypt. The Egyptians retained some of their Egyptian culture but, as obvious, it got mixed with that of the Greeks, Romans, Macedonians, Persians, Syrians, etc.

The new system of astrology that developed in this era is known as *'Hellenistic astrology'*. Obviously, the traditions of Mesopotamian astrology and Egyptian astrology were used in creating this form of astrology. Hermes Trismegistus is considered to be the creator of Hellenistic system of astrology. He is supposed to be the first one in the history of astrology who outlined and described the meaning of *twelve celestial houses* and employed the use of an *ascendant*, thus, giving birth to the creation of *horoscopes* that we are familiar with even today.

The other most notable astrologer of Hellenistic era was Claudius Ptolemy. He mapped over one thousand stars and compiled a list of 48 constellations. Ptolemy is best known for his major work contained in the Four Books of *'Tetrabiblos'*. The first book of *Tetrabiblos* defines the various favourable and unfavourable positions of the Signs and Planets. The second book of *Tetrabiblos* describes as to how and which Planets cause different events on planet Earth. The third book deals with the study of movements and positions of different Signs and Planets at the time of conception and birth of an individual to determine the horoscope. And the last and fourth book of *Tetrabiblos* defines the meaning of the *'Twelve Houses'* of the zodiac. Ptolemy's work has formed the basis of astrology as we know it today and he can be very rightly called the father of modern astrology.

Eventually, the existing names of Planet and Star Gods were replaced with the names of Greek and Roman Gods. The Hellenistic astrology was in practice essentially in its original form until the 7th century CE when Europe entered the Middle Ages. Though, the practice of astrology was hindered in Europe during that period but Hellenistic astrology had already made its way into other parts of the world especially under the influence of Greek and Roman empires.

ARABIAN/PERSIAN ASTROLOGY

When Europe was going through its Middle Ages and with many scholars criticizing the practice of astrology, the development of astrology in Europe was badly hindered. But, the development of astrology remained unimpeded in Asia.

Major observatories were established in Persia and Baghdad for the development of medicine, mathematics, astronomy/astrology, etc. Ulugh Beg, the sultan of Persia, developed the first original star map since Ptolemy in which he corrected the position of many stars and also included many new ones. The Arabs made such tremendous progress in astronomy that even today a great many star names are Arabic in origin and some of them are still used by some astrologers.

While adopting Hellenistic astrology, the Arabian astrologers also developed a new system of astrology known as *'electional astrology'* that was used in everyday affairs such as calculating auspicious time to start a business or inauspicious time to avoid a travel, etc. The Arab astrologers also developed a significant system for divination called *'Arabic parts'* but it is hardly used in astrology now-a-days. The Arabic parts have fascinating names and were believed to influence the life of an individual.

Though Arabs made tremendous progress in astrology but gradually astrology started losing its foot-hold because of the influence of Islam as astrology is forbidden in Islam. There are instances in *Quran* where the Prophet Muhammad has advised against the practice of astrology since he believed that astrology is nothing but a superstition.

WESTERN ASTROLOGY

Western astrology is not basically developed by the European (Western) astrologers as it implies from its name. Actually, the origin of Western astrology lies in the Hellenistic astrology and the Arabian/ Persian astrology. The Hellenistic astrology had made its way into Europe through Greeks and Romans during the 1st century BCE and was in practice until 7th century CE. But when Europe went through its Middle Ages and with many scholars and philosophers criticizing and rejecting the practice of astrology, further development in astrology was hindered in Europe. At that time, the art of astrology was preserved and developed by the Arabian and Persian astrologers. Later on, this whole knowledge of astrology again made its entry into Europe where Hellenistic astrology was being practised in limited form. The basic structure of astrology remained the same but now the formulae developed by Arabian/Persian astrologers and those developed by practising European astrologers were all mixed together to form the present day *'Western astrology'*.

Western astrology is today one of the most known forms of astrology not only in the European countries but almost all over the world. Most people understand this form of astrology as *'Sun Sign'*, or *'Star Sign'* astrology but interestingly many of them don't even know that it is Western astrology. You can come across many people in India who think that it is 'astrology' (Western or Indian - they don't know!). Newspapers and TV channels provide daily information as to what might happen in the life of Aries (people born between 21 March to 19 April). According to Western astrology, Sun passes through the Aries constellation between 21 March to 19 April and thus all people born during that period are supposed to be having the same characteristics as that of the Aries. Most astrologers don't recommend this type of divination and suggest their clients to go for personalized horoscopes for a better understanding of their life and fate.

INDIAN ASTROLOGY

Indian system of astrology (*Vedic or Hindu astrology*) is commonly known as *'Jyotisha'*, though the word *jyotisha* in itself does not convey the actual meaning of 'astrology'. The word *jyotisha* simply means *Gods of Light*, in other words shining visible *Sky Gods*. And the system that deals with these *Sky Gods* is known as *'jyotisha shastra'*. Now, there are two main parts of *jyotisha shastra: ganit jyotisha* (calculative part – can be compared to astronomy) and *phalit jyotisha* (predictive part – it's what we really mean by astrology). *Ganit jyotisha* deals with the study of astronomical bodies – their positions, movements, distance, etc. that leads to the formation of *panchang* (ephemeries). Astrologers need *panchang* to cast a horoscope. *Phalit jyotisha* describes as to what effects Stars and Planets would exert on the life of a subject.

The ancient Indian astrology system was *Nakshatra* (constellations of Stars through which Moon passes during its monthly cycle, also known as Lunar Mansions) based and the zodiac was divided into 28 (later 27) *Nakshatras*. Likewise other ancient civilizations, Indians too believed in many fascinating stories about *Gods of Creation* as well as the *Sky Gods*. One of such stories describes the 27 *Nakshatras* to be the divine wives of the Moon God – *Chandra Dev*.

The location of Moon in the rising *Nakshatra* at the time of birth would mark the authority of the lord planet of that *Nakshatra*. Thereafter, that lord planet would show its influence on the individual and after the period of this lord planet is over, the remaining lord planets would show their influence when their turn comes – it goes into a cycle. This system is known as *'Mahadasha/Antardasha'* cycle and is considered as one of the most important factors in an Indian horoscope.

Apart from the 7 Planet Gods (Sun, Moon, Mercury, Venus, Mars, Jupiter and Saturn), Rahu (ascending node of Moon) and Ketu (descending node of Moon) are also considered as Planet Gods. Here, these 9 Planet Gods are awarded rulership of the 27 *Nakshatras*. Now, the *Nakshatras* have their own properties and the lord planets their own. Based on these properties, the fate of an individual would be decided. The planetary position at birth time was seen with regard to the *'rising nakshatra'* instead of the present day *'rising sign'* system. The influence of planets was also observed as per their position with respect to the specific *Nakshatra*.

Up to the *Vedic* and *Mahabharta* time period, there was no reference of the 12 Signs, 12 Houses and their meaning, etc. Later on, under the influence of different cultures, the traditions of Mesopotamian, Egyptian and Hellenistic astrology were mixed with the *Nakshatra* Astrology. Like Signs where zodiac is divided into 12 equal parts, the Indian astrologers adjusted the 27 *Nakshatras* into 12 Signs in the ratio of 2 ¼ : 1. The 28th *Nakshatra, Abhijit* had to be omitted. Similarly, the 12 Houses and their meaning, lord planets of the Signs and their properties, etc. – all that these newer systems of astrology could offer was adapted into the existing astrology system. Now, the Indian astrologers started casting horoscopes mixed with the elements of *Nakshatra* and Sign Astrology but presently, Indian astrologers give more importance to Signs and neglect *Nakshatras* while making predictions.

Apart from some common features as seen in Indian and Western astrology (12 Signs, 12 Houses, different aspects of Planets, their influence, etc.), the specialties of Indian astrology are: *Dasha* (Planetary effect periods), *Vishesh Lagna* (Special Ascendants), *Varga* (the divisional charts), *Yoga* (the planetary combinations), etc.

The Indian astrology system is the most complex of its time in the present world. Many sub-systems have resulted because of the diverse cultures within the Indian subcontinent. It's amusing to see how most people in India are terrified when they are told by an astrologer that *'Tumhara Shani kharab hai'* (Saturn in your chart is malefic).

CHINESE ASTROLOGY

To begin with, it would not be appropriate to call the Chinese system of divination *'astrology'* since this system is not based on astral bodies. Nonetheless, as it is commonly known today, we may also call the system as *Chinese astrology* for our own convenience. Instead of the 12 Zodiac Signs of traditional astrology, the *'12 animals'* of the Chinese folk-tales take the centre-stage in Chinese astrology which is primarily based on the Chinese calendar, the Chinese zodiac (referred to as 12-year cycle of animals) and the five elements of Chinese philosophy.

Well, let's have a look at the 12 animals of the Chinese astrology:

1. Rat
2. Ox
3. Tiger
4. Rabbit
5. Dragon
6. Snake
7. Horse
8. Sheep
9. Monkey
10. Rooster
11. Dog
12. Pig

Now, let's figure out as to how this system works. In Chinese astrology, each year has its governing *Animal* and *Element*, each month its governing *Animal* and each 2 hour period (24 hours divided by 12 animals) its governing *Animal*. Prediction is made considering these four factors.

Here's an example : Jackie Chan was born at 2:17 pm on 2nd February, 2006. Here, as per Chinese calendar, the year 2006 would be from January 29, 2006 to February17, 2007.

Here, the Element for the Year 2006 is Fire
And the Animal for the Year 2006 is Dog

The Animal for the Month February is Tiger
And the Animal for the Hour (1 to 3 PM) is Sheep

Now, this person may seem to others as having the characteristics of a Dog but the person is a Tiger (internally) and a Sheep (secretively). Element Fire will benefit him in the following contexts: Direction:- South, Season:- Summer, Colour:- Red, Body Parts:- Circulatory system & Heart, Personality traits:- Dynamic, Energetic, Passionate, Enterprising, Adventurous, Restless, Competitive, Leadership skills, Strong and Single-minded. The Element Fire governs Snake, Horse and Goat. So, he'll benefit from people of these signs.

The same rule will apply to individuals born at other times of the year. Here, the place does not matter because there are no astrological charts to be made where the position of stars has to be recorded from a certain place on the earth. All you need is a copy of the Chinese lunar calendar and you can tell all about any individual!

MESO AMERICAN ASTROLOGY

The system used for divination by the people settled in the region of Central America and southern North America, especially the Maya, Olmec, Mixtec, Aztec, etc. is somewhat similar in its approach to the Chinese astrology. There is no such system of tracking the influence of Stars on human beings as is usually seen in horoscopic astrology. So, their system of divination can't be defined as '*astrology*'. But since they were also involved with the phenomena of divination of future, we are discussing them here.

Specific calendars were documented and used for divination purposes. One of the most important of such calendars belongs to the *Maya civilization*. The Maya used two calendars - a 260 day ritual calendar known as *Tzolk'in* and a 365 day solar calendar. Each day of *Tzolk'in* is believed to have some specific character in it. So, obviously it would influence the life of the people born on that day. Interestingly, the 260 day calendar ran parallel with the 365 day calendar and these two calendars came together every 52 years. This 52-year cycle is called a *Calendar round*. At the end of each Calendar round, it was a common ritual to extinguish all fires, break old pots and light a new fire that would symbolize a fresh start.

Recently, in August 2008, many TV channels in India came to know about some sensational findings of the Maya calendar. According to the *Maya Long Count calendar*, the 13th *b'ak'tun* (a repeating cycle of 395 years) ends on 21st December, 2012. Now, this period has great significance for the Maya, for them it's the end of the old-order world for a new beginning. But, all the TV channels kept on terrorising the gullible people of India by announcing that the world was coming to an end in 2012!

CONTRADICTIONS WITHIN INDIAN AND WESTERN ASTROLOGY

In this chapter, we'll discuss Western and Indian astrology as they are the most dominant systems of astrology that exist today. So, first of all, let's get familiar with Indian (in Hindi language) and Western names for Signs and Planets:

Signs:

Western	**Indian**
Aries	Mesh
Taurus	Vrish
Gemini	Mithun
Cancer	Kark
Leo	Singh
Virgo	Kanya
Libra	Tula
Scorpio	Vrishchik
Sagittarius	Dhanu
Capricorn	Makar
Aquarius	Kumbh
Pisces	Meen

Planets:

Western	**Indian**
Sun	Surya
Moon	Chandra
Mercury	Budh
Mars	Mangal
Venus	Shukra
Jupiter	Guru
Saturn	Shani
Uranus	Arun
Neptune	Varun
Pluto	Yam
Dragon's Head (Ascending Node of Moon)	Rahu
Dragon's Tail (Descending Node of Moon)	Ketu

Note: *Rahu* and *Ketu* are considered planets in Indian astrology but not in Western astrology. Sun and Moon are considered planets both in Indian and Western astrology. Uranus, Neptune and Pluto are considered to exert their effects in Western astrology whereas Indian astrologers don't give any importance to these planets (They claim that these planets are too far to exert any effect whereas the Stars of the Zodiac Signs that are millions of times farther than these planets are believed to exert effects!) Scientifically, the status of Pluto as a planet is in question for a long time now. For our convenience, we would mention all planets by the Western names but Dragon's head as Rahu and Dragon's tail as Ketu in the following pages.

Well, forgetting all the criticism by scientists and researchers of the world that astrology is fake, let's just believe for a moment that astrology works. Now, even in that case, there are many contradictions within Indian and Western astrology.

Let's observe the contradictions within Indian astrology first. As we know that India practised *Nakshatra astrology* in the initial stages but after the exchange of cultural ideas with different people at different times in its history such as Babylonians, Greeks, Romans, Arabs, etc., the 12 Signs were gradually incorporated in the Indian astrology.

Now, let's have a look at the properties of Signs in Western astrology:

WESTERN ASTROLOGY: PROPERTIES OF SIGNS

Sign	Polarity	Quadruplicity	Element	Rulership
Aries	Masculine	Cardinal	Fire	Mars
Taurus	Feminine	Fixed	Earth	Venus
Gemini	Masculine	Mutable	Air	Mercury
Cancer	Feminine	Cardinal	Water	Moon
Leo	Masculine	Fixed	Fire	Sun
Virgo	Feminine	Mutable	Earth	Mercury
Libra	Masculine	Cardinal	Air	Venus
Scorpio	Feminine	Fixed	Water	Mars
Sagittarius	Masculine	Mutable	Fire	Jupiter
Capricorn	Feminine	Cardinal	Earth	Saturn
Aquarius	Masculine	Fixed	Air	Saturn
Pisces	Feminine	Mutable	Water	Jupiter

Now, by simply replacing the Western Sign names with Indian Sign names such as Mesh instead of Aries, Vrish instead of Taurus and so on, the property-chart that you get remains the same! How can the properties of both Western Signs and Indian Signs be the same? It clearly shows that either of them has copied the other.

Now, let's compare the Lord Planets of Signs and the Lord Planets of *Nakshatras* in those Signs:

Sign	Lord	Nakshatra	Lord
Mesh	Mars	Ashwani	Ketu
		Bharni	Venus
		Kritika 1	Sun
Vrish	Venus	Kritika 2,3,4	Sun
		Rohini	Moon
		Mrigshir 1,2	Mars
Mithun	Mercury	Mrigshir 3,4	Mars
		Adra	Rahu
		Punarvasu 1,2,3	Jupiter
Kark	Moon	Punarvasu 4	Jupiter
		Pushya	Saturn
		Ashlesha	Mercury
Singh	Sun	Magha	Ketu
		PurvaPhalguni	Venus
		Uttra Phalguni 1	Sun
Kanya	Mercury	Uttra Phalguni 2,3,4	Sun
		Hast	Moon
		Chitra 1,2	Mars
Tula	Venus	Chitra 3,4	Mars
		Swati	Rahu
		Vishakha 1,2,3	Jupiter
Vrishchik	Mars	Vishakha 4	Jupiter
		Anuradha	Saturn
		Jayeshtha	Mercury
Dhanu	Jupiter	Mula	Ketu
		Purva Ashadha	Venus
		Uttra Ashadha 1	Sun

Makar	Saturn	Uttra Ashadha 2,3,4	Sun
		Shravan	Moon
		Dhanishtha 1,2	Mars
Kumbh	Saturn	Dhanishtha 3,4	Mars
		Shatbhisha	Rahu
		Purva Bhadrapad 1,2,3	Jupiter
Meen	Jupiter	Purva Bhadrapad 4	Jupiter
		Uttra Bhadrapad	Saturn
		Revati	Mercury

Note : Rahu and Ketu are awarded the rulership of *Nakshatras* and they also show their influence during their *Dasha* (Planetary effect period). But since in Hellenistic astrology, the lunar nodes are not awarded rulership of any Sign, the Indian astrologers also didn't grant them rulership of any Sign.

In ancient Indian astrology, the zodiac was divided into 28 *Nakshatras*. The position of Moon in any of those *Nakshatras* provided the basis for divination. After the introduction of Signs, the zodiac was to be re-arranged into 12 Signs by incorporating 28 *Nakshatras* into them. But, it was not possible to adjust 28 *Nakshatras* into 12 Signs. Well, 27 *Nakshatras* could be adjusted into 12 Signs in the ratio of 2¼ : 1. So, ultimately *Abhijit Nakshatra* was left out. Now, each *Nakshatra* has further sub-division into 4 parts called as *Charan* such as *Ashwani* 1 *Charan*, 2 *Charan*, 3 *Charan* & 4 *Charan*. In the first Sign Aries, *Nakshatras* were arranged as *Ashwani* 1,2,3,4 *Charan*, *Bharni* 1,2,3,4 *Charan* and *Kritika* 1 *Charan* - that makes it 2¼ *Nakshatras*. Similarly, all the *Nakshatras* were incorporated into different Signs. But, here came the main problem which is still ignored by the astrologers. Lord of Aries is Mars whereas the Lords of the *Nakshatras* in Aries are as: Ketu - *Ashwani*, Venus - *Bharni* and Sun - *Kritika*. Ask an Indian astrologer to explain as to why none of the *Nakshatra* Lords is granted the rulership of the Aries sign in which all those *Nakshatras* are incorporated? The astrologer has no justifying answer. It happens with all Signs except Leo and Pisces and that's mere a chance... nothing more than that!

Moreover, all planets have their individual properties and

effects. Now, which planet lord would affect the destiny of a person born in the Aries sign? For a Western astrologer, it would be easier - Mars. But, for an Indian astrologer, choice becomes very complicated - Mars, Ketu, Venus or Sun? In this way, 12 Signs have 46 planet lords (Leo and Pisces have 3 lords each while others have 4 lords each). Now, there are 12 Houses, each with its own meaning. Planets generate different influence in different Houses and different Signs. Then there are different aspects from different angles and so many different sub-charts: all this leading to more complexity. In an attempt to make prediction, there are so many factors and probabilities that prediction itself becomes 'ridiculous'.

Above all, the most distinguished feature indicating that *Nakshatras* were incorporated into Signs is that there is no similarity between the shapes (assumed) of Signs and *Nakshatras* in those Signs. For instance, Aries contains the following *Nakshatras* - *Ashwani*, *Bharni* and *Kritika* 1 *Charan*. Here, the assumed shape of *Ashwani* is that of the *face of a horse, Bharni* the shape of *vagina* and *Kritika* the shape of a *knife*. Well, is there any similarity between the shape formed by these *Nakshatras* and the shape of a sheep? So, on what basis the ancient Indian astrologers incorporated these *Nakshatras* into Aries? The same mismatch can be seen in the shapes of all Signs and *Nakshatras* in those Signs.

So, we can well understand that while adapting Signs into *Nakshatras*, the ancient Indian astrologers messed up with the ancient astrology of *Nakshatras*. Well, for the modern Indian astrologers, the *Nakshatras* don't make much difference as they hardly consider the influence of *Nakshatras* in a horoscope. They simply go the Western way - Ascendant, Signs, Lord-Planets, their position and aspects with respect to different Houses and Signs, etc. and with their own indigenous sub-charts, *mahadasha/anterdasha* (planetary effect periods), etc. Nonetheless, they use *Nakshatras* for various other purposes - horoscope matching for marriages, calculating 'auspicious' times for marriages, starting new businesses, shifting to a new home, journeys, etc.

Now, let's have a look at the contradictions within Western

astrology. Most Western astrologers use *tropical astrology* which is based on the idea that astrologers of the Hellenistic era defined the Star Sings according to the seasons in which the Sun rose in them. When astrology was being developed by the Babylonian, Egyptian and Hellenistic astrologers around 1000-100 BCE and the astrological formulae were being formulated, the Sun actually was in the Aries constellation at the vernal equinox from 21 March to 19 April. But due to the phenomenon of 'precession of equinoxes' over a period of so many centuries, Sun no longer passes through Aries during that period. On the other hand, the actual position of Sun in Aries now is from April 19 - May 13 and it remains from March 12 - April 18 in the constellation of Pisces! The same fact applies to the position of Sun in all Signs. And, the position of Sun in different Signs will keep on changing because of the shifting of equinoxes by one degree about every 72 years. So, after ascertaining one's actual Sign, one will have to check after every 72 years as to whether they belong to the same Sign or not! As a result of this 'precession of equinoxes', everybody is getting absolutely wrong idea about their Sun Signs. In simple words, people born during the period (21 March to 19 April) don't belong to the Aries sign (which they think) but to the Pisces (which they don't know). And if you thought you were a Libra, you are wrong, you are a Virgo instead! Now, to ascertain your actual Sun Sign, you have to consult an astronomer who would show you the actual position of Sun in different Signs during the year. It's needless to say that the phenomenon of 'precession of equinoxes' has completely undermined Western astrology.

Few Western astrologers and most Indian astrologers use *sidereal astrology* where in the astrological signs approximately align to the sky constellations of the same name. They criticize the tropical approach as 'totally useless' as it does not align with the actual position of the stars. They also point out the absurdity of applying Northern hemisphere seasons to the whole planet when there are now large populations within the Southern hemisphere who experience seasons six months apart from those in the North.

Well, it would be important to mention here that instead of the 12 constellations as assumed by the ancient astrologers, scientifically, Sun passes through 21 constellations. In other words, if it goes by assuming the shapes so formed by the Stars, there are 21 astronomical constellations of the zodiac. So, may be the ancient astrologers could have derived divination from the 21 constellations instead of just 12. Nonetheless, it's just an assumption of shapes (could have been any shape) and could have been any number (12 .. 21 .. 31) - doesn't matter at all!

Amazingly, despite all these blunders, astrology still works!!!

EFFECTS OF STARS AND PLANETS ON HUMAN LIFE

Unfortunately, just like the ancient humans who worshipped Stars and Planets, there is no dearth of modern humans who still believe in the same practice. However, with new scientific discoveries and inventions, some avoid calling these Stars and Planets as 'Gods' but still believe that cosmic rays being emitted by them are affecting their life in some way or the other.

The modern astrologers just like the pre-scientific era astrologers leave no space for criticism of astrology. They very proudly highlight the occasions when predictions made by them came true. But, when pointed towards numerous others which failed the test of time, they always come up with some sort of excuse or justification. If you persist and want explanation, you'll be charged more, of course for their time, and eventually shown the door after being labelled an 'unbeliever'.

Astrologers often boast the fore-fathers of astrology to be the first real scientists of the world - who calculated the cycles of different planets, observed their motions, calculated the motions of the Moon and its relationship to the sea tides, who discovered the relationship of the Sun with the different seasons and climate on Earth, who discovered that the Sun takes 365 days for one revolution around the Earth (now when it's been proved otherwise, they can still argue and justify the biggest 'fake belief' of astrology prevalent before Galileo for thousands of years).

Well, there is no denying the fact that astrology has been one of the most important of the ancient sciences. When we call astrology 'science', we mean by its pure scientific side known as 'astronomy'. From Indian point of view, astronomy means '*Ganit Jyotisha*' and astrology means '*Phalit Jyotisha*'. And, when an Indian scholar says that astrology is scientific, he's actually talking about '*Ganit Jyotish*' i.e. astronomy while also impliedly justifying '*phalit jyotisha*'. Anyhow, in an effort to understand the effects of different Planet and Star Gods, the ancient astrologers made tremendous progress in astronomy and mathematics.

Interestingly, except from slight changes in the magnetism and gravitational pull from the Sun and Moon with respect to Earth's position during different periods of the year, no other effect from any astronomical body on planet Earth and its inhabitants has been observed by the scientists so far. Moreover, the effect of Sun and Moon is only of physical nature and applies to all alike. To think that Sun selects Aries for giving warmth and Libras for giving coolness on a bright sunny day is in itself the biggest folly but that's how the believers in astrology think. Moreover, to think that during the period of Venus (if it's exalted in a horoscope), one would get fame, money, etc. - list of such endless beliefs - is one of the biggest plights of modern humans.

The Sun's distance from earth is about 150000000 kilometers, if calculated in terms of distance travelled by light in one second; one can say that the distance of Sun from Earth is 8 minutes and 5 seconds i.e. Sun rays reach Earth in 8 minutes and 5 seconds. It implies that Sun is not there where we see it now but was there 8 minutes and 5 seconds before! The distance of Moon from Earth is about 382400 kilometres which implies in terms of Moon's virtual and real position that Moon is not there where we see it now but was actually there I.3 seconds before! Saturn's distance from Earth is about 1268847480 KM which implies that Saturn is not there where we see it now but was actually there 1 hour and 11 minutes ago. After Sun, the nearest Star to Earth is Alpha Centauri which is about 4.3 light years away i.e. approximately 40000000000000 KM (roughly 250000 times more distant than Sun) which means that it was there 4 years and 3 months ago but we are seeing it now! And, many Stars of the prevailing Sun Signs are even 100's of times more distant than Alpha Centauri! We know Sun's effect on Earth or for that matter Moon's effect as they are comparatively quite near to the Earth. But any effect of the astronomical bodies thousands and millions of times more distant than Sun and Moon is simply out of question and merely a superstition of the ancient humans. When astrologers don't consider the effects of Planets like Uranus and Neptune, how can they consider the effects of Stars that are millions of times more distant than these Planets?

Moreover, astrologers generally give excuses when their predictions don't come true that the horoscope might not be correct because of wrong recording of birth time (even by margin of a single or few seconds). Now, when the astronomical bodies are not actually in those positions on the basis of which horoscopes are cast, how can astrologers even think or claim the validity of a horoscope? This is really the most absurd folly of astrology and at least on the basis of this single folly, astrology should be denounced. I mean when the astronomical bodies are not in those positions which astrologers use for casting horoscopes but were actually there 1 second, 1 minute, 1 hour, 1 day, 1 month, 1 year or we don't know how many years ago, how can astrologers justify that virtual position of astronomical bodies is good enough basis for casting a horoscope when (according to them) even a single-second mistake in recording birth-time can result in the casting of an in-correct horoscope!? Actually, the more you research the validity of astrology, the more you find about its invalidity.

Note: Distance of astronomical bodies from Earth keeps on changing according to Earth's position with regard to them during different periods of the year.

Kindly consult a Science book for detailed knowledge about the effect of astronomical bodies on planet Earth and its inhabitants.

TESTS UNDERTAKEN BY RESEARCHERS

Astrologers all over the world claim that astrology works, if that is the case, then there must also be some principles under which astrology works. And the validity of those principles could also be tested. But when they are asked to take a test and prove that astrology works, they make excuses and shy away from the test!

Going by the claims of the astrologers, many scientists and researchers undertake the task of testing the validity of astrology from time to time. In the coming chapters, I have given some tests (undertaken by researchers all over the world) without making any changes in the original text so that I may not be accused of 'misrepresenting the facts'.

But before you go through those tests, I want to highlight the compelling life story of Mr. Rudolf H. Smit, who practised astrology from 1972 to 1984 and authored many articles and studies on astrology. But while practising when he realized that astrology doesn't actually work and is merely a superstition, he was so shocked that he underwent clinical depression for some years and that even cost him his marriage. Thereafter, he abandoned his astrological practice and started conducting scientific research on astrology.

In 2000, Mr. Smit founded the website 'www.astrology-and-science.com' which is supported by his collaborators (mainly research authors) namely Hubert Basler, T Patrick Davis, Geoffrey Dean, Suitbert Ertel, Jacques Halbronn, David Hamblin, Ivan Kelly, Bart Koene, Alan Leo, Arthur Mather, David Nias, Peter Niehenke, Garry Phillipson, and Koen Van de moortel. Mr. Smit and his collaborators deserve my heartiest thanks and good wishes for their good work. Without the research work of such people, this book would not have been possible.

Here's the story of Mr. Smit as given in the following web link '**www.rudolfhsmit.nl/a-pass2.htm**':

"Astronomy has been part of my life since I was a boy of nine growing up in several towns and cities in the Netherlands. In our living room there was a big bookcase, and since my parents were not so fond of novels, it contained above all popular scientific works. One of

these books was titled Mijn Sterrenwacht [My Observatory]. It was a lucid account by P.G. Meesters, one of the well-known Dutch amateur astronomers of that time (I am talking about the 1930s and 1940s).

Thanks to his enthusiastic writings I became an ardent amateur astronomer. I began asking my parents not to give me toys for my birthdays but, instead, books on astronomy. When I was 12 years of age, I had already about 20 books on astronomy and quite a few of them contained pretty heavy stuff.

Anyway, virtually all of those books had one thing in common: They told readers that although astrology was once an offshoot of astronomy, in our modern times it has no basis in scientific fact, therefore its practitioners are, at best, gullible but well-meaning people or, at worst, hopeless and dangerous charlatans.

Since I was only 12 or so I was quite willing to believe what all those illustrious authors had written, so I sincerely believed that astrology was hogwash and astrologers were dangerous charlatans. And if anybody at the time would have said "mark my words, you will soon be an astrologer yourself, and an ardent defender of astrology at that", no doubt I would have thought "you must be nuts".

But although nobody had ever pronounced such a prophecy, it did happen anyway. This is the story of how it all began, how it unfolded, and how it ended in disaster.

My Story Begins

It was 1968 and in that year I became technical editor of a journal on photography. My immediate boss was the editor of this journal. He was an academic with a distinguished background in chemistry and (photographic) education. A highly critical and erudite, warm and humorous person for whom I soon developed great regard.

But one day, this same man said something that made my stomach turn in disgust. The director of our publishing company had come into our office, apparently with the only purpose to blow off steam -- he was grappling with a problem, but could not decide what to do, and so on, and so on. When he had left, my boss said: "See, a typical Libra, finds it hard to make decisions". I could not believe my ears and was horrified. My boss, an academic of some standing, was daring to say such silly things! So I pulled out all the stops and argued that this was all nonsense, because the stars were too far away to exert any physical influence whatsoever on human lives, and so on, and so on.

My boss listened to me patiently and then asked: "have you ever studied the subject?" I was utterly astounded: "Of course not, why would I waste my time with such silly stuff?!" His answer was: "If I were you, I would devote some of your time to astrology, because only then can you start to judge it properly."

I discover that my Sun Sign fits me

This was a crucial moment in my life, because I realised that he was as right as one could be. I was judging with lots of authority something I had no real knowledge of. This kind of attitude is, indeed, quite irresponsible and also somewhat reprehensible.

So, in the end I overcame my disgust and bought myself a booklet about my Sun Sign. It was from a series of twelve booklets written by the well-known French astrologer Andre Barbault. And yes, I have to admit that much of what I read did seem to accurately describe me. I was truly astonished. Inspired by this unexpected positive outcome, I made the relatively simple calculation for the Ascending Sign, which as a matter of fact seemed to be right on the cusp between two signs. I bought Barbault's description for these two signs, and yes, it seemed to be "me" again! (Actually the consecutive sign seemed to fit me better and a year or so later I found out that it was in fact my Moon Sign. So there you are!)

But at that point some skepticism crept in. What if I would buy all the other nine star sign booklets? I took a personal bet that after reading those booklets I would discover in each of them descriptions that would fit me. And indeed, so it occurred, although I had to admit that the fitting descriptions were not equally divided over all twelve signs. That is, some signs fitted me much better than others. In any case, it was reason enough to shelve the lot for a while. This all happened in the late 1960s.

And so does my horoscope

But then I happened to visit the parents of someone I knew. In their living room was a big bookcase, and having in mind the famous adage "show me your books and I know who you are" I began inspecting the content of this bookcase, and soon discovered two text books on astrology. Pleasantly surprised I asked the couple which one of them was interested in astrology. The woman confirmed her interest, and she and I had a brief exchange which led to her promise to cast my horoscope. Two days later I found in my mail a nicely drawn up horoscope figure, as well as a few written lines, which made me feel flabbergasted. She had written things which were quite specific to my character and situation in life, and which she could not have known.

But I was still not fully convinced. So I did something else: I sent my birth data to a well-known astrologer and asked him to write an analysis purely based on those data, hence without ever seeing me. Six weeks later I received his nicely structured, six-page description which fitted me miraculously well. I was elated and the die was cast: from now on astrology had me firmly in its grip! This was the beginning of an exciting time.

In those years astrology text books were fairly hard to come by, but after some searching in shops for secondhand books I found a few and also an ephemeris. Next I taught myself the casting of horoscopes, and of course the first thing I did was casting my own. Again, there was that wonderful feeling of having encountered a miracle.

The elation of seeing astrology work

But I did not limit my investigations to my own horoscope. Virtually everyone else in my circles became victim of my thirst for knowledge about astrology. I asked them to provide me with their birth data, calculated and drew up their horoscopes on the spot, and began to interpret them using the recipes in those old text books. To my great satisfaction virtually everyone agreed with "their" descriptions. Occasionally even the profession of such person was written up in the textbooks! This was truly astonishing, and I felt elated.

It went further and further. During 1975 and 1976 I even wrote articles on astrology for the popular magazine Aarde & Kosmos [Earth & Cosmos], which were re-published in November 1976 in a book called De Planeten Spreken [The Planets Speak]. It included what

I thought at the time was good evidence for planetary influences such as the findings of Gauquelin, and had over 300 pages.

To cut the story short, I had sought contact with the few astrologers that, at the time, were active in the Netherlands, and found out that in particular one of them was making predictions of the worst kind and with dire consequences, namely that his clients got upset and so terrified with fear that they had to seek help elsewhere. I felt that this was highly unethical, and I decided to mobilise the few good professional astrologers I had met, and asked them to help me set up what was to become the NGPA, the first Society of Practising Astrologers in the Netherlands. In other countries such as Britain and the USA, similar societies concerned with ethics had been existing for many years, but until now in the Netherlands there had been little concern.

My astrological handbook for beginners

Not only would this society make sure that its members would deal with their clients in a truly professional manner, but their behaviour in this regard would be based on a properly designed ethical code. And so it happened. This society was founded in 1977 and I was appointed its first chairman. I also wrote an astrological handbook for beginners and became founding editor of the magazine of NVWOA, the Dutch society formed in 1976 for the critical study of astrology.

A wonderful time followed. Everybody was full of optimism and felt that it would be only a matter of a few years before astrology was fully accepted by society. As for my own astrological endeavours, I had set up practice as a part-time professional astrologer and was receiving many clients, so the future looked rosy. It turned out greatly different.

Being right with the wrong charts

It was in this period (around 1978) that I had my first major mishap. I had a client, let us call her Ms Johnson, for whom I did a reading. All seemed to go pretty well; she was nodding all the time while saying, "Yes, yes, you are so right" or words of a similar meaning. But then I said something like: "well Ms Johnson, we...."

She interrupted: "Sorry, my name is Petersen, not Johnson." I then experienced a terrible sinking feeling, because I then saw before me the horoscope of a Ms Johnson, but the person before me was surely not this Ms Johnson! Apparently I had taken the wrong chart from my file cabinet!

Truly, I have forgotten how I got myself out of this most embarrassing terrible mess, but apparently I had managed the situation pretty well, because she went away a happy client.

After seeing her out I sat in my study, confused thoughts racing through my mind. How is it possible to do a correct reading based on a wrong chart? Did not all text books tell us that a horoscope is unique, that is, only fitting its native and no one else? If so, how on earth could I have made correct delineations based on a totally wrong chart? I was completely puzzled. In the end I let the matter rest, but from now on I was on the alert! And not without any reason because a few years later, a similar mistake occurred to me, but then I noticed it in time.

My dormant skepticism re-awakens

In any case, it won't come as a surprise that from that moment onward the skeptic who had been dormant within me for several years, was about to wake up again. No matter that I had many clients whose satisfaction was loudly proclaimed after I had done an astrological reading for them. Despite all this positive feedback I felt that I could not trust any longer the astrological text books I had consulted. They were too often in disagreement.

As a matter of fact, my whole attitude towards astrology was gradually changing to the extent that I was becoming a pain in the neck for my fellow astrologers. I was now critical of the "anything goes" attitude of so many of them, and of how they tended to believe anything that prominent astrological authors had written, be they ancients or from more recent times. For example, whenever I questioned a particular astrological statement, their response tended to be: "It is so, because (famous author) says so." (Note the present tense: says so, not said so, even when the famous author had been dead for many years!) If I asked: "how does he know?", they replied "well, er, by experience". If I then asked: "Experience, based on what? On empirical research?", their eyes usually went blank.

Enter the computer

It was also the time (the final three years of the 1970s) when the first home computers entered the scene. I bought one of them, the Commodore PET 3032 (a forerunner of the later famous C64) and the astrological software for it was developed by a friend of mine, who had also bought such a machine.

Thanks to this machine and its software I was able to test a multitude of horoscopes on a great variety of astrological statements found in astrological text books. It took me a number of years to carry out these projects. I succeeded, but to my great chagrin the test results were contrary to all hopeful expectations. One did not have to be a professional statistician to find out that many, if not all, statements in astrological text books, fell flat when tested on a great number of horoscopes.

For example, I tested the statement that in the charts of people who had died an accidental death, there would be a remarkable incidence of Progressed Ascendant to Mars, or of Progressed Mars to the Ascendant. Sure, there were a few (but the word says it all: a few), hence not an overwhelming number which could confirm the text book statement. And so it went on and on. And one can imagine that my views on astrology had sobered down somewhat. Yet, I was still a believer, simply because I had happy clients, who tended to come back. So why complain!? Until the day when the penny dropped.

I meet Geoffrey Dean

In February 1984, I met face to face with Dr. Geoffrey Dean, a man whose researches into astrology were already having an impact on the astrological scene. In 1979 I had bought a copy of the book Recent Advances in Natal Astrology that he had compiled with Arthur Mather and many others, and was deeply impressed by it since, for one thing, its findings corroborated my own investigations.

Anyway, we both had been invited to lecture at the yearly conference of the Federation of Australian Astrologers, and I took the opportunity to ask him to stay at my home. (Since 1980 I was living near Melbourne where I took on the agency for Matrix software until 1985.) We had many inspiring discussions and during those he showed me a fairly thick packet of paper; in fact, a long draft article on astrological counseling that he was circulating for comment. In it he had brought together much relevant information taken from orthodox sources (it had 87 references) that was almost never found in astrology books. It also incorporated comments on two previous versions from about a dozen astrologers and psychologists.

He asked me whether I was willing to give it a thorough read and then forward my comments. Of course I agreed. Accordingly, shortly after Dean had left for his home town Perth in Western Australia, I began reading this paper. As usual his writings were highly informative. One chapter though gave me that terrible sinking feeling again.

Not because he had written something wrong, but because there was the sense of immediate awareness that he was so right! And that was the moment when the penny dropped. The sudden realisation how I had been doing my readings and why I had been so successful. And that was not thanks to astrology, but instead thanks to various things that I seemed to be pretty good at. Let me explain.

The art of 'Cold Reading'

The chapter that affected me was called Chartside Manner: Nonastrological Factors in Personal Validation. In this chapter Dean discussed about 20 factors that affect "personal validation" or the way a client personally assesses or validates an astrological reading (The number of factors later reached 34, see Artifacts in reasoning on this website under Doing Scientific Research). These factors included things like the Barnum effect (seeing specifics in generalities) and selective memory (ignoring errors), most of which I did recognise, that is, I had the strong feeling that indeed I myself had been a victim of most of them. However, the things that gave me that terrible sinking feeling were the effects described under "Cold Reading", and now I quote Dean in full:

"Cold Reading Effects, or how body language tells the story. Here the reader uses non-verbal cues (e.g. pupil dilation and hand movements) leaked by the client to hone in on the truth. In a counselling session a great deal of non-verbal communication goes on, often without anybody being aware of it, so obviously it pays to give added weight to what is sensed. [Dean later told me that "paralinguistic cues" (the tone and loudness of the voice, and the effect of anxiety on

the voice owing to constriction of the throat muscles), can be just as important as non-verbal cues.]

"The intuitive astrologer will attend to client reactions automatically, which helps to explain why many astrologers claim that intuition is important for maximising accuracy.

"The key points of Cold Reading are as follows :

1. *Watch the eyes and hands for signs that they say yes and no*
2. *Make the reading happy and positive*
3. *Be a good listener*
4. *Loosen the client's tongue with flattery*
5. *Discover the problem and then tell the client what they want to hear*

"Of course an astrologer may be using Cold Reading without knowing it. Neher [here there is a reference to The Psychology of Transcendence, McGraw-Hill 1980] concluded from observations of astrology/palmistry/tarot/etc readers that they were often 'astute, sensitive individuals who pick up subtle clues leaked by the client. Usually neither the reader nor the client is consciously aware of this communication process, which therefore can result in a reading that seems mysteriously perceptive.'

"The point is that a skilled Cold Reader can produce a totally convincing reading very similar to a chart reading (and probably more accurate) but without using a chart. In that case, it cannot be claimed that astrology plays an essential part in the reading process."

The penny drops

Well, apparently, but without ever having been consciously aware of it, I had been an excellent Cold Reader -- which is what I realised on that fateful day in February 1984. It was mainly thanks to these Cold-Reading skills and to my unfailing desire to help my clients that I had an excellent rapport with them, and thus had sessions which were, almost without exception, successful in the sense that both my client as well as myself were happy. So, the only good thing supplied by astrology was the beautiful mandala called horoscope and its symbols. The rest was due to my being caring, attentive to the client's needs, and sensitive to what Dean calls the client's "paralinguistic and non-verbal cues".

Now it also became devastatingly clear why I had excellent sessions based on the totally wrong chart. Sympathy, Cold Reading, and the nice astrological symbolism had done the trick, not astrology itself. Conclusion: A warm, caring, perceptive reader can work with any chart, hence also the wrong chart. Thus, in reality, I had been dealing with a beautiful and perfect illusion. Yes, perfect and grandiose, but an illusion, no matter how beautiful, remains an illusion.

My happy world of astrology collapses

This harsh realisation, on top of all the negative statistical results of the many serious studies (including my own) into astrological claims, had a devastating effect on me. My happy world of astrology collapsed. It felt as if the bottom had been kicked away from under my existence.

This was the beginning of a terrible time. First of all, due to this awful new knowledge that it all had been an illusion, I felt compelled to close my astrology-practice. After all, I had been dealing in illusions, and hence felt it unethical to continue selling such illusions.

If that had been all, it would not have been so bad. But since astrology had been my great passion, which now all of a sudden had turned into a great disappointment, it was as if I had fallen into a big black hole. When trying to look forward, I saw no horizon, no future. I had invested my whole existence on the rosy promises of astrology, and on its certainty that one's life has a definite meaning and is inseparably linked with the universe. But now I saw only a terrible never-ending blackness. A clinical depression ensued which would last for some years and which, for one thing, cost me my marriage.

Only after I had returned to the Netherlands in 1987 and had to find a way to begin a new life (I found a new wife and a good job) did my sorrow about the loss of astrology slowly fade away.

I was not alone

It was little consolation that I was not alone in discovering that astrology was an illusion. When I was living in Perth I visited Geoffrey Dean many times, and he showed me letters his clients had sent him when he was a practising astrologer in the late 1970s. They said things like "very accurate" and "so true it is amazing" and "you know me inside out". One letter I remember especially was from a lady client who had found an hour or so of chart reading more helpful than six months of psychiatry, and voluntarily doubled his fee. His clients were every bit as happy as mine had been.

Then in 1980 he found to his amazement that clients were just as happy with a reading that was the opposite of the authentic reading. Like me he had discovered that any chart would do provided the astrologer is sensitive and caring. And like me he immediately stopped reading charts for money. Later I discovered that one or two other astrologers had abandoned their astrological practice for the same reason as I had (for example David Hamblin, a former Chairman of the AA, see 'Astrology as Religion' under Philosophy). So I was not alone.

A new beginning

It seems to happen quite often that people who have lost a belief, whether it is a religious belief or say a belief in astrology, tend to develop a revulsion against their former conviction. Not so with me. Astrology still has my interest, but the focus is now mainly on the big question why astrology still exerts so much attraction to so many people. In other words, why do astrologers still go on believing whereas the evidence against it is mounting and mounting?

I have discussed this question at length in my article Moment Supreme, where I conclude that astrologers go on believing because the apparent match between horoscope and client is such an extremely persuasive situation that it is easy for them to ignore every evidence against astrology -- as indeed it seems they have always done.

Other factors may also apply depending on the astrologer. Thus astrology has undeniable appeal, and satisfies the longing of many people to be part of an all-encompassing whole, to feel part of the universe as a living entity, and to know that one's life has a definite meaning since it is part of that living entity. For is this not exactly the Big Question for most people -- has my life meaning, why am I here, where am I going? For many, and that included me, astrology seems to provide an answer. My devastation when I discovered that this answer was a Grand Illusion should therefore not come as a surprise.

The pleasures of astrology re-visited

I have learned to live with this sobering knowledge. And, in addition, I have set up my own website (Astrology-and-Science) which is a fountain of knowledge for all those people, astrologers and skeptics alike, who wish to know more about recent scientific findings about astrology. In contrast to what hostile skeptics do, we (that is, my collaborators and myself) do not ignore the good side of astrology. We simply supply the facts as they are. And as regards astrologers, we do not consider the great majority to be charlatans, since most astrologers tend to be nice people whose only sincere desire is to genuinely help their clients.

As for me, after twenty odd years I have taken up again the reading of charts (now and then, that is), if only to experience again the wonderful feeling when such a reading turns out to be successful. However, I am not asking money for such sessions, and I tell my new "clients" in advance that I am offering them a Grand Illusion, which may be helpful nonetheless. If it is helpful, it is not because astrology itself is helpful, but because astrology sets a scene that helps me to be helpful.

Well, I am sure that you have fully enjoyed reading Mr. Smit's thought-provoking story. You can log on to 'www.astrology-and-science.com' for many interesting and educating articles on scientific testing of astrology.

Now, let's look at some tests undertaken by researchers worldwide.

TEST NUMBER 1

Source: www.rudolfhsmit.nl/a-murd2.htm

Kansas City Committee for Skeptical Inquiry (KCCSI) sent one of their members (say Peter) to five astrologers posing as a man interested in working with young people. Peter gave each astrologer the birth time, date and place of John Gacy (one of the worst convicted serial killers in American history) instead of his own, plus a computerized natal chart from a company internationally recognized for accuracy (Neil F. Michelsen), and asked them for their advice. The astrologers unanimously encouraged him to persue youth work and none could see any problem with this.

(John Gacy was born in Chicago on 17 March 1942 at 00:49 CST, or 05:49 GMT, CST being the time required by Illinois for birth registration even though War Time was then in effect. Some hospitals did not follow this rule, so the actual birth time might have been an hour later at 06:49 GMT. Both times give a Sagittarius ascendant.)

At the time, the real John Gacy was being held on death row at Menard Correctional Center in Chicago. He received 12 death sentences and 21 life terms for the brutal torture and murder of 33 young men and boys. He was executed by lethal injection on 10 May 1994.

Gacy was selected for the test because his chart should portray a clear picture of a sadistic sexually motivated killer. If astrologers are able to spot personality traits and destinies in any chart, then this is one they should have no trouble with.

The way in which Gacy murdered his victims was particularly repulsive. They were usually teenage boys whom he lured into his home and overpowered. He had a pair of trick handcuffs, which he would demonstrate that he could slip out of. After immobilizing them by persuading them to put on the handcuffs, he repeatedly raped and tortured them. Finally, after they begged for their own deaths, he would strangle them, often by shoving their own underwear down their throats. Each astrologer was asked to examine the computerized chart for as long as they wanted before giving their reading.

Advice given by the astrologers

John Sandbach, a nationally known astrologer who has authored six books, advised Peter not to "become weighed down with regrets about how you could have done more in some past situation". He described a "plasticity or lack of aggression" in the chart and encouraged Peter to work with young people because he could "bring out their best qualities".

Local astrological talent, Randy Goodman, was reported by the Kansas City Star (April 10, 1985) to have investigated "mysterious flying hotdogs" at the Radisson Hotel Muehlebach. He told Peter that he was "really born to serve people." He stated that "In the past you have used your energies very well, so therefore in this life you have a lot to contribute, and... your life will be very, very positive."

Another local astrological celebrity, Norma Knight, was also given an opportunity to analyze the chart. She described Peter as "a very, very sensitive person." When asked whether a youth ministry would provide suitable employment, she replied "I think that you can be very good with kids and that it might be a good medium for you to learn to be more trusting in the giving and receiving."

Beverly Farrel lays claim to being an "internationally recognized author, lecturer and teacher of religion, metaphysics, astrology and psychic awareness" with "30 years experience in the field of (the) paranormal." She also encouraged the man behind the chart to go into youth work, because "when you're working with young people you're not gonna have a lot of heavy-duty problems."

The results seemed to indicate that astrologers cannot read a person's character from the positions of the planets at the moment of birth, nor can they see into anyone's past or future, nor do they seem to possess any insights other than the ability to impress their clientele.

TEST NUMBER 2

Source: www.rudolfhsmit.nl/a-murd2.htm

Joyce Jillson, whose column is carried by the Tampa Tribune and who is Hollywood astrologer to the stars, unwittingly allowed ABC-TV reporter John Stossel an opportunity to demonstrate for his millions of Good Morning America viewers in November 1988 just how well astrology works in spite of it appearing not to be real.

Jillson (who normally charges $200 per chart) first prepared a detailed reading for a person unknown to her, whose birth information (which is all she requested) was supplied to her by Stossel. Stossel then distributed a copy of the completed horoscope to each of 20 students in an adult education class. Each student had given Stossel their own birth information one week earlier.

The students, thinking they were each reading their own personalized horoscopes, marvelled at how Jillson knew things about them that no one else could possibly know. Typical responses were "very accurate", "I am amazed", "hits points that nobody knows." Stossel asked one student "is it you?" (yes) "but is it different from other people?" (yes it is). But the students, male or female, were reading the same horoscope, that of someone described by Jillson as "enormously bright... (with) sexual charisma... great charm... a sense of moral propriety... (who) may know celebrities..." Jillson's reading, supposedly unique, was clearly a one-size-fits-all unisex reading.

Stossel felt that Jillson may have incorrectly assumed the birth information to have been his own. In fact, it was that of mass murderer Edward Kemper III, who in addition to many other "charming" deeds had cut off his mother's head and used it as a dartboard. Ironically one statement fitted the authentic subject quite aptly, namely "takes life seriously." Concluded Stossel, confronting Jillson on camera with the facts, "I just think this shows it's a hustle, and you make money by writing general things that everybody believes is about them."

All this had no noticeable effect on Jillson's popularity. In 2003 she suffered what the Skeptical Inquirer Nov/Dec 2003 page 9 called "the ultimate embarrassment for an astrologer." In her syndicated column of 12 Sept 2003, Jillson had given a glowing horoscope of TV star John Ritter "having a Virgo Sun sign helps keep his career ticking", even though he had died the day before.

TEST NUMBER 3

Source: www.psychicinvestigator.com/demo/AstroSkc.htm

Astrologers who claim they can analyze a person's character and predict a person's life course just by reading the "stars" are fooling the public and themselves, University of California researcher Shawn Carlson has concluded in a unique double-blind test of astrology published in Nature (December 5, 1985). The controlled study was designed specifically to test whether astrologers can do what they say they can do. Carlson, a researcher at UC's Lawrence Berkeley Laboratory, found astrologers had no special ability to interpret personality from astrological readings. Astrologers also performed much worse in the test than they predicted they would, according to Carlson.

The study refutes astrologers' assertions that they can solve clients' personal problems by reading "natal charts," individual horoscopes cast according to the person's date, time, and place of birth. "It is more likely that when sitting face to face with a client, astrologers read clients' needs, hopes, and doubts from their body language," said Carlson, who is also a doctoral candidate in Physics at UCLA and a professional magician who has himself performed "psychic ability" demonstrations.

Carlson's research involved 30 American and European astrologers considered by their peers to be among the best practitioners of their art.

The study was designed specifically to test astrology as astrologers define it. Astrologers frequently claim that previous tests by scientists have been based on scientists' misconceptions about astrology.

To check astrologers' claims that they can tell from natal charts what people are really like and how they will fare in life. Carlson asked astrologers to interpret natal charts for 116 unseen "clients." In the test, astrologers were allowed no face-to-face contact with their clients.

For each client's chart, astrologers were provided three anonymous personality profiles - one from the client and two others chosen at random - and asked to choose the one that best matched the natal chart. All personality profiles came from real people and were compiled using questionnaires known as the California Personality Inventory (CPI). The CPI, a widely used and scientifically accepted personality test, measures traits like aggressiveness, dominance, and femininity from a long series of multiple-choice questions.

According to Carlson, the study strenuously attempted to avoid anti-astrology bias by making sure astrologers were familiar with the CPI and by incorporating many of the astrologers' suggestions. At the same time, to prevent testers from inadvertently helping astrologers during the test, the project was designed as a double-blind study where neither astrologers nor testers knew any of the answers to experimental questions.

Despite astrologers' claims, Carlson found those in the study could correctly match only one of every three natal charts with the proper personality profile - the very proportion predicted by chance. In addition, astrologers in the study fell far short of their own prediction that they would correctly match one of every two natal charts provided. Even when astrologers expressed strong confidence in a particular match, they were no more likely to be correct, Carlson found.

Concludes Carlson:

We are now in a position to argue a surprisingly strong case against natal astrology as practised by reputable astrologers. Great pains were taken to ensure that the experiment was unbiased and to make sure that astrology was given every reasonable chance to succeed. It failed. Despite the fact that we worked with some of the best astrologers in the country, recommended by the advising astrologers for their expertise in astrology and in their ability to use the CPI, despite the fact that every reasonable suggestion made by advising astrologers was worked into the experiment, despite the fact that the astrologers approved the design and predicted 50% as the "minimum" effect they would expect to see, astrology failed to perform at a level better than chance. Tested using double-blind methods, the astrologers' predictions proved wrong. Their predicted connection between the positions of the planets and other astronomical objects at the time of birth and the personalities of test subjects did not exist. The experiment clearly refutes the astrological hypothesis.

"A lot of people believe in astrology because they think they have seen it work," Carlson observed. He believes many astrologers are successful at their art because they draw important clues about clients' personalities and lifestyles from facial expressions, body language, and conscious or unconscious verbal responses. "When magicians use the same technique, they call it 'Cold Reading'," said Carlson.

Based on his scientific findings, Carlson suggests many people would do better to spend their money on trained psychology counselors. However, he disagrees with those who would like to see astrology outlawed. "People believed in astrology for thousands of years and no doubt will continue to do so no matter what scientists discover. They are entitled to their beliefs, but they should know that there is no factual evidence on which to base them."

"The astrologists' reactions so far have been pretty much what I expected," Carlson told the SKEPTICAL INQUIRER. "The astrologists whom I didn't test are saying that the test was not fair because I did not test them. Of course, if I had tested them instead, and they had failed, then the astrologers I actually tested would now be saying that the test was not fair because I did not test them.

"I attended an NCGR party - I was the only non-astrologer in the house - to discuss the research shortly after it was published. The discussion was, to put it politely, energetic. I have not yet received a serious scientific challenge to the paper." The newsletter of the American Federation of Astrologers Network published a response in January (1986). "I was very disappointed to see that it largely consists of personal attacks," Carlson said. He said its few substantive criticisms are attributable to ignorance of his experiment, of the CPI, and of basic scientific methodology.

Carlson's study was supported by Richard Muller, professor of Physics at UC Berkeley, and paid for by a general congressional research award.

TEST NUMBER 4

Source: www.rationalistinternational.net/article/20030827_1_en.htm

A detailed scientific long-term study by researchers in Britain proves the central principle of astrology invalid and baseless. It puts an end to the fantastic old claim that the constellation of stars and planets at the time of birth could influence or even determine the development of an individual's character and course of life.

The "Time Twin Study" was started in London in 1958 as a medical research project. Registering more than 2,000 babies, born within minutes of each other on a day in early March, it had the objective to compare the time twins' health development. The field of investigation was soon extended. The research team monitored the test persons over several decades, recording observations about more than 100 parameters in connection with health, occupation, marital situation, anxiety level, aggressiveness, sociability, IQ levels, abilities in music, art, sport, mathematics, language, etc. They tried to collect evidences for similarities between the 'time twins'. However, no similarities could be identified.

"The test conditions could hardly have been more conducive to success but the results are uniformly negative", stated Dr. Geoffrey Dean, astrologer turned scientist from Perth, Australia, in a report about the study, published in the current issue of the Journal of Consciousness Studies. Carrying out an analysis of the study, Dr. Dean and his colleague Prof. Ivan Kelley, Psychologist at the University of Saskatchewan, Canada, found that there was no special trait or tendency shared by the 'time twins'. They were just as different as people born on any other day under any other planetary constellation.

The claim that stars and planets could influence character and life of human beings has long been dismissed by rationalists and scientists as there is according to all known scientific principles no kind of mechanism imaginable by way of which this influence could possibly work. Here is empirical proof that it does not work at all. The study shows clearly that astrological predictions based on the coordinates of birth do not correspond with reality. They are nothing but exercises in deception.

This should be the end of one of the oldest superstitions. But it is not hard to predict that the show will still go on. There are obviously too many people, who like to be deceived and too many, who make enormous money by deceiving them.

TEST NUMBER 5

Source: http://arumugam.tripod.com/blueplanet/astrology.htm

Dr. Abraham T. Kovoor (1898-1978) was free thinker, rationalist and psychiatrist from Kerala, South India who later spent his life in Sri Lanka. He was the president of the Rationalist Association of Sri Lanka where he and the renowned Professor Emeritus Carlo Fonseka held regular meetings at Thurston College, Colombo. He came to the conclusion that there was absolutely no objective truth behind such claims and beliefs in all types of alleged psychic, para-psychological and spiritual phenomena based on his intensive scientific researches for over half a century. He was one of the first and the only scientist among psychical researchers in the world at that time to be awarded a doctorate for his research by the Minnesota Institute of Philosophy of U.S. for his thesis on psychic and para-psychic phenomena.

Here's brief account of Dr. Kovoor's work as given in the above-mentioned web link:

"In his article under the caption "Is Astrology Scientific?" published in the Sunday issue of the Times of India, Mr. V.V. Bhujle makes an effort to convince the readers that astrology should not be condemned as a superstition until it is proved so by empirical tests. He is prepared to accept astrology as a true "science" because it was believed all over the world from ancient times, and among the believers there were and are eminent scientists. In support of his belief in astrology Bhujle writes:-

It may be noted that in the 14th century a number of universities in Western Europe, among them Paris, Bologna and Florence, had chairs of astrology... Astrology is regaining a large popular following... Educated people in the West, especially in the United States, ask each other what sign they were born under. Astrological literature is flourishing as never before... It is difficult to deny the fact that there are many scientists and investigators who are quietly gathering astrological data and testing them in various fields... And the possibility that astrology may as well undergo a transformation from the traditional view to the modern empirical one cannot be ruled out... Carl Jung endorses the validity of astrological phenomena. Professor Jung certainly knew the origin and anatomy of superstitious beliefs better than those scientists who brand astrology as nothing more than a superstition... There was never a scientific attempt made to substantiate the statement that astrology is an exploded superstition... Before astrology can be condemned, its validity or otherwise should be empirically tested."

False Concept

Mr. Bhujle should realise that a false concept will never become right just because the majority of people believe it or because it is believed from ancient times, or because there are eminent scientists among the believers.

Astrology originated when man's knowledge of astronomy and the universe was wrong. Hence, astrological calculations were and are made on wrong data. Of the nine planets (navagraha) of astrology only five are real planets. Of the remaining four, one is a star and another a satellite. The remaining two do not exist at all! How can conclusions derived from wrong data be true?

Astrological charts are prepared according to the relative visual positions of the so-called planets in the twelve zodiacal constellations at the time of the birth of a person. As the solar planets and the zodiacal stars are millions of miles away from the earth their visual positions at any moment are only virtual and not real. In preparing the chart for a person, astrologers make use of the wrong virtual positions of the planets. If they have the knowledge and ability to calculate and find the real positions of the planets through astronomical calculations, perhaps astrologers themselves will lose faith in their cult! Since light from planets and stars takes several minutes to millions of years to reach the earth, it is clear that astrologers' charts are wrong by several minutes to millions of years!!

Blind belief in astrology on the ground that Newton and Carl Jung believed it is as absurd as drinking urine as a curative medicine on the ground that Morarji Desai did so!

Mr. Bhujle says that it is the responsibility of scientists to prove their negative statements concerning astrology. It was exactly for this purpose that I included astrology and palmistry among the 23 items of my fifteen-year-old permanent challenge, and offered an award of one lakh Sri Lankan rupees to those who could make 95 percent or more correct predictions in a test to be conducted by me. Although I do not share Bhujle's view that it is the duty of a scientist to prove or disprove things that do not exist, I ventured to do so because astrology and palmistry have become a curse to society like all other superstitions. Can Mr. Bhujle persuade a single astrologer or palmist to face my test? I have conducted this test on many occasions, and found that astrologers and palmists cannot make better predictions than laymen who can only guess!

Latest Exposure

The latest empirical test on astrology and palmistry I conducted was on February 12, 1978.

On reading a news item in the Ceylon Sunday Observer that a Sri Lankan, who has a flourishing business in London as a fortune-teller, succeeded in finding oil in Ghana by looking at the palm-print of the President of Ghana, I wondered whether the Government of Sri Lanka could make use of this man, while he was on a holiday here, to locate oil in Sri Lanka by looking at the palm of President Mr. J.R. Jeyewardene! Provoked by this fictitious and fantastic claim I challenged through the same paper this palmist-cum-astrologer Mr. Cyrus Abeyakoon and all other astrologers and palmists in Sri Lanka to face a test I proposed to conduct at Thurstan College Hall on February 12, 1978. To make it attractive for them I offered to pay my usual award of one lakh rupees to those who get 95 percent or more correct answers. Some of those who advertise regularly about their ability to make correct predictions from dates of births or palm-prints also were invited by letters to take part in the test.

Four fortune-tellers responded and informed me that they would be coming to take part in the test. A fifth person telephoned me and said that he would like to demonstrate publicly his power of healing through prayers to Jesus Christ. Since faith-healing was one of the 23 items of my permanent challenge, he too was asked to come.

Thurstan College hall was fully packed with spectators on February 12, long before the scheduled time. Sharp at 5 p.m. the proceedings started with a preliminary talk by me about the origin and evolution of witchcraft and occultism, and the reason why I had to throw out a permanent challenge against all those who claimed occult and miraculous powers. Thereafter astrologers and palmists were asked to come on to the stage and take their seats. Only one palmist and the faith-healer came up although there were several fortunetellers in the hall! I am sure readers will be intelligent enough to understand why those fellows who earn rupees five and ten from the public by telling their fortunes rejected my offer of one lakh! Knowing very well that they had no chance of winning my award, they did not want to risk their future practice by exposing their bluff!!

A layman from the audience was requested to come up and take his seat with the others. First I introduced the faith-healer to the audience, and then requested him to keep on praying to remove a black mole at the base of my nose, while I got on with the test on palmistry. I could have asked him to pray to Jesus to heal the cancer in my bladder. But, since there was no possibility of showing the result to the audience without conducting a biopsy, I preferred the former.

While the prayer of the faith-healer was going on, I pulled out two sealed envelopes from my file. One of them contained the palmprints of both palms of ten persons prepared at my request by the Sri Lankan police, and a similar sealed cover containing the identity of the ten persons with their sex and whether they were alive or dead, attested by a responsible police officer. The other sealed cover contained a sheet of paper giving the dates and times of birth, correct to the minute, of ten persons together with the latitudes and longitudes of the places of their birth. Another sealed cover contained the necessary information about the sex and longevity of the ten persons, attested by the respective living persons, and close relatives of the dead.

I broke open the seal of the first cover before the public, and gave the ten numbered palm-prints, first to the palmist and later to the layman, they were asked to mark on papers supplied which of them were males, females, dead and living.

Two journalists from the audience were called up to the stage to mark the correct answers by comparing with the attested copy supplied by the police officer. The palmists got 30 percent and the layman 20 percent correct answers. Had I called a few more laymen to take part, at least some of them would have got even 50 percent. Any fool could have got that much!

The black mole at the base of my nose, and the one lakh of rupees are still safe with me. I am keeping the sealed cover containing the birthday data of the ten persons unopened to be used on a future occasion.

Wide publicity given in local paper about the result of this test had a very healthy effect. Many fortune-tellers in Sri Lanka had to close shop due to want of patronage. Even by this type of exposition it is difficult to exterminate this type of parasites because still there will be gullible fools to consult them.

The Oxonian Prime Minister of Sri Lanka Mr. S.W.R.D. Bandaranaike, postponed his oath taking ceremony by 30 minutes at the advice of his "family astrologer". Although he took his oath at the "auspicious" time, he was assassinated before he could complete his term. Still Presidents and Prime Ministers of Sri Lanka and India will continue to take their oaths only at auspicious times fixed for them by quacks!

B.V. Raman

Just before my 4th "Divine Miracle Exposure Campaign" in India I wrote to Dr. B.V. Raman of Bangalore, who has earned a fortune through his Astrological Magazine, requesting him to attend any of my lectures in Bangalore to take up my challenge and show to the people of India that correct predictions could be made through astrology.

Although I spoke at 8 public meetings in and around Bangalore, he came to none of them. He was intelligent enough to know the danger of facing a scientific test! Can Mr. Bhujle persuade Raman or any other "genuine" astrologer to take up my challenge?"

Mr. Bhujle, who says, "There was never a scientific attempt made to substantiate the statement that astrology is an exploded superstition" can himself carry out a similar test on B.V. Raman and get convinced about the myth of this ancient cult.

Well, such was the personality and vision of Dr. Abraham T. Kovoor. I wish India had produced more gems like him.

TESTS UNDERTAKEN BY THE AUTHOR HOROSCOPIC ANALYSIS OF FAMOUS/INFAMOUS TEST SUBJECTS

Tests undertaken by the Western researchers intrigued my doubts about the validity of astrology. Well, I must confess here that while browsing on the internet I was very upset not to find any similar tests undertaken by the Indian scientists/researchers. Moreover, I was hoping to find some *Indian astrologer-turned-critic* of astrology but found none. The only reference I got in this context was that Indian scientists had protested against the decision of University Grants Commission to provide funds for courses in Astrology and Palmistry at Indian universities. But, shamefully, their protests yielded no result and after some time, they surrendered.

Anyway, to start my research, the first thing I needed was to collect birth information for my test subjects: Nationally and Internationally known people (popular as well as notorious). Getting birth data for International subjects proved much easier than the Indian subjects. The reason being that the Westerns have maintained many websites devoted to astrology that don't shy away from sharing the birth information of renowned people whereas websites maintained by Indians hardly give any birth information. So, for getting birth information about Indian subjects I bought as many astrology magazines as possible. Apart from Indian and International subjects, I collected charts of some people I personally knew. Overall, I prepared horoscopes for 24 celebrity and 9 non-celebrity subjects.

Utmost care was taken while preparing charts. All the factors that could cause an incorrect chart have been taken care of - like while preparing the chart of a person born in a Western country, you need to know whether it is Standard Time or Daylight Saving Time, accordingly you have to check the correctness of latitude and longitude. If in a chart, ascendant changed within 5-6 minutes, that chart was deleted from the "research list". Almost in all the charts of my subjects, ascendant doesn't change in at least 15 minutes. So, there is no scope of any excuse by the astrologers who claim that "things change in seconds". I have given them the margin of 900 seconds!

Now, with everything arranged, I started my research from Jammu (my hometown) and obtained readings for my test subjects from astrologers practising in different parts of India such as Jalandhar, Ludhiana, Kurukshetra, Delhi, Mathura and Gokul. Overall, I obtained 101 readings for the 33 test subjects between the period of December 2006 and February 2007.

Well, it wasn't easy to get the astrologers to read the past of the subjects. The astrologers are only interested in predicting the future events. If emphasized to tell the past events, they become suspicious and hesitate in reading on the pretext that they don't have much time and that other 'troubled souls' are waiting for their 'help'. So, after some initial readings, I got an idea. I took the astrologers into confidence that I have my own set up of astrology business - an office and an internet-connected computer which gets me regular orders for casting and interpretation of Vedic horoscopes from clients all over the world. I convinced them that I didn't have time to learn the predictive part of astrology (since it's a very detailed study) as I have other businesses to look after too. I made a lucrative offer to the astrologers to get into some kind of partnership where we would be mutually benefitted - like when the rich foreign client is convinced, I would arrange all 'astrological remedies' through them and thence we would share the profits. I impressed upon them that we cannot dream of getting rich by dealing with miserly Indian clients who are not good pay-masters and often look for free services. On the contrary, cash-rich foreigners could happily part with their money for our services. I further suggested my fellow astrologers that we could open some branch in USA and other rich Western countries so as to earn 'big dollars' and also enjoy respect from 'troubled souls' there. Almost all the astrologers liked my business ideas and must be wondering now as to where I've disappeared after promising them 'big dollars' and an '*ashram*' (kind of a spiritual centre) in Hollywood!!!

Coming to the readings - for the national and international celebrity subjects, I changed their names but kept the same horoscopes of my known subjects (though I have changed their names in this book for the sake of their privacy). The subjects were posed according to their age - some as my friends and some as my relatives.

Please note that Western names of planets will be used except for *Rahu* (Dragon's head) and *Ketu* (Dragon's tail). Kindly also note that date of birth of Test Subjects mentioned in this book is in the following order :- Date - Month - Year.

Also note the meaning of following terminology for your reference:

Mahadasha: Planetary Main-period

Antardasha: Planetary Sub-period

Mantra: a set of certain words for worshipping, praying or invoking a deity

Japa : chanting mantra

Havan: ritual ceremony where specific number of mantras are chanted while making offerings to Planet-Gods through the God of Fire (*Agni Dev*). These ceremonies are often performed by priests.

Yog: combination of different planets

There are many words in Hindi language (related to astrological stones and rituals) that can't be translated into English. The meaning of those words can be, somehow, guessed in the context they are written.

For example: by '*Rudrabhishek* worship recommended for 11 days', one can understand that '*Rudrabhishek*' is a sort of religious service and has to be performed for 11 days.

By 'Wear *Lahsunia*', one can well understand that it is an astrological stone.

Now, let's see what astrologers predicted about the test subjects (names in alphabetical order).

ARNOLD SCHWAZENEGGER as Robert Baily

Birth: 30-07-1947 at 4-10 AM (DST), Graz, Austria

Source: www.astrolreport.com
www.astrotheme.fr
www.zodiacal.com

Arnold is an Austria born champion bodybuilder-turned Hollywood action film hero-turned US politician.

Arnold first tasted success at the young age of 18 when he won Mr. Europe Junior title. In 1967, he became the youngest person to ever have won Mr. Universe title. He has won five Mr. Universe awards overall. In 1968, Arnold immigrated to USA where he won seven Mr. Olympia awards while acting in Hollywood movies at the same time. He rose to international stardom after the release of 'The Terminator' in 1984 and since then has been regarded as one of the most successful action heroes of all times.

For his passion to serve people, Arnold joined politics as a Republican. He was elected the Governor of California first in 2003 and for the second time in 2006. Arnold got married in 1986 and has four children.

HOROSCOPIC ANALYSIS

Jammu Astrologer:

1. Lot of travels and bad tastes (especially regarding women and wine)
2. Clever, good diplomat and bureaucrat
3. Mars not good - bitterness in married life, unfaithful to wife
4. Extravagant - bad planning in money matters
5. No scope in politics
6. September 2006 to February 2010 - crucial time, planning not fruitful
7. July 2007 to January 2009 - problems in married life
8. Death due to heart attack before even making his will
9. *Rudrabhishek* worship recommended for 11 days

Delhi Astrologer:

1. Business-minded: Electronics, Computer, Cloth, Finance, Consultancy, Agency related business
2. No good relation with parents
3. Eye related problem in young age
4. Long life but has many enemies
5. *Kaal Sarp Yog*: struggling life
6. *Mangalic* (certain inauspicious position of Mars in a chart): Less happiness in married life - divorce or death of wife possible
7. Second marriage possible after performing "*Swayamvar Vivah*" (sort of ritualistic marriage)
8. Lucky stones: Emerald, White Sapphire
9. *Gandmool* worship required
10. Worship *Ganesh* (Hindu God)
11. Feed *laddoos* (Indian sweet) to the beggars on Wednesdays

Gokul Astrologer:

1. *Bhadra Yog*: makes him a great soul
2. Saturn-Sun combination: not good for family life
3. *Angarak Yog*: prone to heat reaction related diseases
4. *Kemdrum Yog*: very inauspicious, always worried due to financial crises
5. *Kaal Sarp Yog*: can cause him imprisonment very soon
6. *Wear Kaal Sarp* locket or perform ceremonial worship as soon as possible

AMITABH BACHCHAN as Rajat Malhotra

Birth: 11-10-1942 at 4-05 PM, Allahabad, India

Source: Jyotish Sagar - January 2006
Soubhagya Deep - November 2006
Sadhna Path - December 2006
www.astrodaily.com

Amitabh Bachchan is one of the most acclaimed Indian actors of all times. While shooting for 'Coolie' in 1982, he survived fatal injury and was hospitalized for months together.

Bachchan had a brief brush with politics as well - he was elected a Member of Parliament in 1984 but being unable to cope up with the political games, he resigned in 1987. In 1996, Bachchan formed his film production company 'ABCL' which ran into high losses, bringing him to the verge of bankruptcy. But, Bachchan still stands tall in the Indian Film Industry.

In 1999, Bachchan was named the "Greatest Star of the Millennium" by BBC online poll where he defeated many Hollywood legends such as Alec Guinness, Marlon Brando, Sir Laurence Olivier and Charlie Chaplin. In 2000, he became the first living Asian to have been immortalized in wax at London's prestigious Madame Tussauds Wax Museum. He got married in 1973 and has two children.

HOROSCOPIC ANALYSIS

Jammu Astrologer 1:

1. Education level should be normal
2. Siblings 3 to 5
3. No cooperation from parents
4. Disputes with wife
5. Bad habits in life - wine and women
6. Dissatisfaction from children
7. Service class
8. Average life style and status in society till the age of 50

9. *Maha Mrityunjaya Japa* (astrological ritual for avoiding major threat to life) to be performed after 30 December 2006 to safeguard against ills of drinking problem
10. Donate green cloth, green vegetables and green gram until 2006
11. Wear *Lahsunia*
12. Chant "*Aum Pran Prin Proun Sah Shanaye Namah*"

Jammu Astrologer 2:

1. Malefic Venus has indulged him in all kinds of bad habits especially alcohol
2. No success in art line - only wastage of time and money
3. Should concentrate on film distribution instead of acting or direction
4. Two marriages are very much possible and may be already has a secret 'wife'
5. Overall not so successful in life
6. Should do partnership with Taurus or Gemini Sign people
7. Lucky numbers are 1,3,7 and 9
8. Should strictly avoid numbers 5 and 8
9. Blue Sapphire recommended

Mathura Astrologer:

1. Position of the lord of 'Children House' in 8th House indicates worries from the children side
2. From 30-12-2006 to 28-5-2007: sub-period of Ketu in main-period of Ketu indicates deterioration in wife's health, financial crisis, many ups and downs in life
3. From 28-5-2007 to 28-7-2008: sub-period of Venus in main-period of Ketu indicates betrayal from friends
4. *Maha Mrityunjaya* and *Mrit Sanjivni japa* required
5. *Aum hon jun sah*: chant this mantra yourself or appoint a priest
6. Ketu's period can be destructive - chanting Ketu mantra for 125000 times can avoid bad period

7. Ketu can also be pleased by chanting Ketu mantra for 1000 times before silver or gold-plated fish and thereafter by offering the fish to the sea
8. If interested in appointing us, fee is Rs.250000 (half for the Mathura astrologer and half for me)

Kurukshetra Astrologer:

1. Family life not good - bad relations with wife and children
2. *Bandhan Yog* will keep his success confined according to *Lal Kitab* (in English it would mean "Red Book" - this book also contains astrological formulae)
3. Lord of 10th House in 8th House - no progress in business
4. Prone to allergies
5. Ketu in ascendant means mental disturbances
6. Exalted Jupiter in Enemy House indicates betrayal from family and friends
7. Lord of Fortune in 8th House - problems with regard to good luck
8. No *Pitra Dosh* and *Kaal Sarp Yog*
9. Favorable businesses - Grocery Store, Confectionery Store, Agency related business
10. Bad period for one and a half year started since 28th October 2006
11. Feed cows daily
12. Worship *Ganpati* and *Shivji* (Hindu Gods)

AJAY DEVGAN as Gaurav Sharma

Birth: 02-04-1970 at 2-25 PM, Mumbai, India

Source: Jyotish Sagar - January 2006

Son of a veteran stunt director, Ajay Devgan surprised the nation with his entry in his first film when he rode on two bikes with his legs on each one of them. He is a National Film Award winning actor and holds a good position in the Indian Film Industry. He got married in 1999 and has one daughter.

HOROSCOPIC ANALYSIS

Jammu Astrologer:

1. Playboy nature
2. Moody type
3. Pays less importance to father and vice versa
4. No social standing
5. Jupiter of 4th House is malefic
6. Venus, Mars and Saturn in 10th House - many ups and downs in professional life
7. Sub-period of Jupiter in main-period of Jupiter from February 1993 to March 1995 - no professional success
8. From 1995 onwards - made money but all went to drains
9. December 2000 onwards - more interest in sensual enjoyment
10. Jupiter-period ends in February 2009 and Saturn-period starts: good time from February 2009 to February 2012
11. Recommended Stone: Blue Sapphire

Ludhiana Astrologer:

1. No status in society
2. Problems with father, mother and wife
3. Saturn is malefic - February 2009 to February 2012 (sub-period of Saturn in main-period of Saturn): more problems in life
4. Loss of money, troubles in family life, some frustrating litigations, etc.

5. Despite efforts, there would be less success
6. Financial survival difficult till the age of 50
7. Should chant Saturn *mantra* for betterment in life

Mathura Astrologer:

1. Should be very lucky - lord of ascendant in 7th House is giving full glance to the ascendant
2. Less compatibility with siblings
3. Rahu in 8th House makes him suspicious that someone has cast 'black magic' on him, bad dreams, betrayal from friends possible
4. Malefic Saturn in 10th House - many ups and downs in business, problems from government side but Mars in own Sign will lessen bad effects of Saturn
5. Lord of Fortune, Jupiter, in 4th House will give benefits but there would be some physical ailments too
6. From 1995 to 1997: sub-period of malefic Saturn in main-period of Jupiter - downfall in business
7. From 1997 to 2000: sub-period of Mercury in main-period of Jupiter - bad time
8. From 2000 to 2003: sub-period of Venus in main-period of Jupiter - good time
9. From 2003 to 2004: sub-period of Sun in main-period of Jupiter - bad time
10. From 2004 to 2005: sub-period of Moon in main-period of Jupiter - normal time
11. From 2005 to 2006: sub-period of Mars in main-period of Jupiter - good time
12. From 2006 to 2009: sub-period of Rahu in main-period of Jupiter - mentally upset
13. Chances of divorce especially before May 2007
14. Worship *Vishnu* during Jupiter-period

BILL GATES as Jim Gray

Birth: 28-10-1955 at 10-00 PM (ST), Seattle, Washington, USA

Source: www.astrolreport.com
www.astrotheme.fr
www.astrologysoftware.com

Bill Gates (William Henry Gates III) co-founded Microsoft, computer software company, in 1975. The company made him so rich that he has been listed as the richest person of the world for 15 consecutive times. Currently, as of April 2009, he again stands at number one position. In 2000, Bill founded 'Bill & Melinda Gates Foundation' that provides charities for social causes. He has also authored and co-authored several books. Bill has been named as one of the 100 people who most influenced the 20th century by Time magazine. He got married in 1994 and has three children.

HOROSCOPIC ANALYSIS

Jammu Astrologer:

1. Long Life
2. Religious minded
3. Un-settled in business
4. Married life in danger, take precautions until the middle of 2008
5. Second marriage possible
6. Two daughters
7. No financial aid from father
8. For success in politics, wear Blue and Yellow Sapphire otherwise Diamond
9. *Kaal Sarp Yog*: problematic but can be rectified here in India without personal visit, send photo and fee

Jalandhar Astrologer:

1. Ketu in ascendant will cause diseases
2. Rahu also not favorable: family problems
3. Sun not favorable: less respect in society

4. Happiness from children
5. Ups and downs in business to remain
6. *Kaal Sarp Yog*: worship silver-made *Naag-Nagin* (pair of Cobra snakes, considered as deity in India)
7. Saturn worship required for protection against enemies

Mathura Astrologer:

1. Ketu in ascendant and Rahu in the House of Spouse: divorce very much possible
2. Less happiness from children
3. 1 February 2007 to 18 February 2007: more problems in married life
4. Consider second marriage after 18 February 2007
5. Sub-period of Jupiter in main-period of Sun to remain from 27-9-2006 to 16-7-2007: financial position not good, consider partnership
6. Lord of 4th House, weak Sun, in 6th House: less will power against enemies
7. During the sub-period of Ketu in the main-period of Sun i.e. May 2009 to September 2009: mental state very upset like that of a mad person
8. Jupiter is the lord of 11th House as well as 8th House: financial condition always bad
9. Saturn worship recommended
10. Make two male-figures of wood, cut from a *chikra* tree: worship one and wear the other as locket

BRITNEY SPEARS as Ciara Lohan

Birth: 02-12-1981 at 1-30 AM (ST), Mahon, Mississippi, USA

Source: www.khaleda.com
www.zodiacal.com
www.astroprofile.com

Britney Jean Spears is one of the most controversial and famous American pop singers and holds the record for best selling teenage artist. She's named as the most searched person on the internet in the Guinness World Records book edition 2007 and 2009.

Britney's first marriage in January 2004 was annulled just after 55 hours! The same year in September, she married again and the following year gave birth to her first son. Her second son was born in 2006 but in 2007, she got divorced. Unfortunately, Britney has been suffering from mental disturbances for quite some time now and partly due to this fact, she was denied custody of her sons and has only visitation rights.

HOROSCOPIC ANALYSIS

Jammu Astrologer:

1. Profession: service class
2. Two marriages: second marriage successful
3. First marriage: 2008 to 2013
4. Second marriage: after 2013

Delhi Astrologer:

1. Long life and good health
2. Good job and good reputation
3. High middle class life style
4. Suitable professions: Fashion designing, Artificial jewelry, Art, Painting, Advertising, Media, etc
5. First child: boy
6. Second marriage successful
7. *Kaal Sarp Dosh*: problematic in life, rectification recommended

Ludhiana Astrologer:

1. Less help from father
2. Good relations with mother and siblings
3. Possibility of chest problems
4. Angry and stubborn
5. Venus not favorable: no success in Music
6. Within eighteen months starting from December 2006: marriage to a very rich person
7. *Kaal Sarp Yog*: needs rectification
8. Favorable stones: Pearl, Blue Sapphire and Yellow Sapphire
9. Should donate her used clothes
10. *Trikhand Yog*: 125000 *japa* recommended

BENAZIR BHUTTO as Zareena Bano

Birth: 21-06-1953 at 9-00 PM, Karachi, Pakistan

Source: Soubhagya Deep - November 2006
www.zodiacal.com
www.astrotheme.fr

Un-deterred by the execution of her father, deposed Pakistan premier, late Mr. Zulfikar Ali Bhutto, the charismatic late Benazir Bhutto re-organized her father's party 'Pakistan Peoples Party' and won 1988 elections to become the first woman to head the government of a Muslim majority country at age thirty five.

After being dismissed by the then-President of Pakistan under charges of corruption, her party lost the elections held in 1990. In October 1993, elections were again held, which were won by the PPP coalition, returning Benazir to office until 1996, when once again her government was dismissed on corruption charges.

Benazir and her husband, Mr. Asif Ali Zardari, were charged with corruption and faced a number of legal proceedings. They have three children. Mr. Zardari spent eight years in prison and was released in 2004. Benazir spent most of this period in exile and returned to Pakistan for participating in general elections but was assassinated in an election rally in December 2007.

HOROSCOPIC ANALYSIS

Jammu Astrologer:

1. Good aspect of Jupiter: professional life very good
2. *Mangalic*: divorces in two marriages, third marriage successful
3. No Star favoring political success
4. Will live away from birth place
5. Success in South Pakistan
6. Venus-Moon aspect: latest technology related business is beneficial
7. Prone to piles problem

8. Good times after 27 March 2007

Delhi Astrologer:

1. Stubborn nature
2. Incomplete education
3. Financial problem from 31-10-2006 to 10-9-2009
4. Maternal wealth disputed
5. Touring type work, Trading or Manufacturing, Ready made garments, Fashion designing related business
6. More than one marriage - reunion with present husband very difficult
7. Will slowly become spiritual
8. Saturn remedies: feed black dogs, donate black gram to a mosque/temple, black blankets to the poor, bananas and jaggery to monkeys

Gokul Astrologer:

1. Stars not favorable for good health: *Navgrah Shanti* recommended
2. Avoid partnerships in business
3. Mars in 7th House causing delay in marriage: Mars rectification required
4. Problems in business until 2008: Rahu rectification required

PRINCE CHARLES as Brad Delson

Birth: 14-11-1948 at 9-14 PM (ST), London, England

Source: Jyotish and Vaastu - August 2004
www.astrolreport.com
www.zodiacal.com
www.astrotheme.fr

Prince Charles, the Prince of Wales, is the eldest son of Queen Elizabeth II and Prince Philip, Duke of Edinburgh, thus, first in line to the British throne.

The Prince's marriage to late Princess Diana, in 1981, made headlines of most of the newspapers in the world. Their marriage always remained in the focus of media attention until the couple finally divorced in 1996. Unfortunately, Princess Diana died in a car accident the following year. They have two sons. In 2005, Prince Charles got married to his old time friend, Ms Camilla Parker Bowles.

The Prince of Wales is well-known for his extensive charity works, particularly for the Prince's Trust. He also carries out a full schedule of Royal duties and is increasingly taking on more Royal roles from his aging parents.

HOROSCOPIC ANALYSIS

Jammu Astrologer 1:

1. Can do business and service together
2. Engineering, Electronic goods related business
3. Income from Army or Defense duty
4. Between the age of 23 and 25 years - problem in mother's health
5. Marriage in 25th year - problems in married life
6. Three children
7. Happy go lucky type
8. Bald, toothless, weak eyes
9. Health problems from 1995 to August 2006

Jammu Astrologer 2:

1. Rahu-Moon *Yog* will create illness
2. Malefic Sun (till 2009) will create problems in government affairs
3. Should be doing private job
4. Moon period starts after 2009 - good period
5. No scope in politics or high official post
6. Malefic Venus has indulged him in bad habits
7. *Raj Yog* after 2013
8. Overall a middle class life style
9. Normal relationship with wife and kids
10. Should have 3-4 siblings
11. Major achievement in life after the age of 60 years
12. Diamond recommended

Delhi Astrologer:

1. Good nature
2. Stomach problems to remain
3. Affairs with ladies but married life still good
4. Business reasonably good
5. Time generally good until 2008
6. Pray to God before air travels
7. Avoid black clothes and goods
8. Use white and yellow clothes/goods more
9. Recommended stones: Pearl and Yellow Sapphire
10. Rahu worship must be performed

Gokul Astrologer:

1. Cool nature
2. Good education
3. Family life good, happily married
4. Rahu-Moon combination causing *Grahan Yog*: relations not good with father and children
5. Money wise normal: Saturn in the House of Wealth causing loss instead of profit
6. Stone: Blue Sapphire
7. *Navgrah Shanti* recommended

FAROOQ ABDULLAH as Lokesh Koul

Birth: 21-10-1937 at 12-30 PM, Kashmir, India

Source : Tantra Darshan - July 2006

Farooq Abdullah is son of the famous Kashmiri leader, late Mr. Sheikh Mohammad Abdullah. Sheikh Abdullah spent many years in jail as a result of his continued struggle for Kashmir against Indian aspirations. Anyhow, he also got the opportunity to head the State of Jammu and Kashmir (India) on three different occasions.

Farooq, though a doctor of medicine by profession, preferred to benefit from his father's political stature and joined his party 'National Conference'. He has served as Chief Minister of Jammu and Kashmir on three occasions till date. He is married and has three daughters and one son, Mr. Omar Abdullah.

HOROSCOPIC ANALYSIS

Jammu Astrologer:

1. Good married life
2. Good relations with children but if children need due share in property, they have to perform *havan*
3. May 2004 to October 2006: health problems
4. Jupiter in ascendant: no scope in politics since politics is generally a dirty game and Jupiter doesn't allow one to join politics
5. Saturn rectification recommended

Delhi Astrologer:

1. Long life
2. Wife had an abortion or miscarriage
3. One boy and one girl
4. Stomach related problems
5. Jupiter in ascendant: honest, kind, religious
6. Malefic Sun will cause bad reputation
7. *Raj Yog*: high administrative job but no success in politics

8. *Gaj Kesari Yog*: will bring laurels to family name
9. *Mangalic*: but no major problems with wife
10. Financially sound
11. Recommended stones: Pearl and Yellow Sapphire, never wear Ruby
12. Sun worship, *japa, havan* required

Gokul Astrologer:

1. *Hans Yog* and *Bhadra Yog*: great soul
2. High posts: especially related to judiciary, should be a Judge
3. Malefic Sun: not a dominating personality, less influential
4. Malefic Venus and Mars-Venus aspect: bad character
5. Not very good relation with sons but they will get due share in property
6. Girls more than boys
7. Saturn in 4th House: submissive to wife
8. Sub-period of Venus in main-period of Saturn until 20-5-2009: very bad period - chances of heart attack
9. Wear Blue Sapphire or Saturn locket
10. *Maha Mrityunjaya japa* to be performed

GEORGE BUSH as Brian Edward

Birth: 06-07-1946 at 7-26 AM (DST), New Haven, Connecticut, USA

Source: Soubhagya Deep - July 2006
www.astrolreport.com
www.khaldea.com
www.astrodatabank.com

George Walker Bush served as the President of United States of America on two occasions, in 2000 and 2004. Following the terrorist attacks on America on September 11, 2001, Bush declared a global war on terrorism and ordered the invasion of Afghanistan to overthrow the Taliban, destroy Al-Qaeda and to capture Osama bin Laden. In March 2003, Bush launched attacks on Iraq, asserting that Saddam Hussein had developed weapons of mass destruction but non-existence of such weapons caused Bush and his close ally, Mr. Tony Blair (former British Prime Minister) both national and international condemnation. Bush is married and has two daughters.

HOROSCOPIC ANALYSIS

Jammu Astrologer:

1. Some problems in business but it's better to keep doing the same business
2. No political success
3. Two marriages in life
4. 2nd Marriage between October 2007 to March 2008

Delhi Astrologer:

1. Saturn in ascendant: breathing related diseases
2. September 2006 to August 2009: better time
3. Should be a widower
4. No savings in life but lavish lifestyle
5. No success in politics
6. Mentally confused
7. Recommended: Coral and Yellow Sapphire

8. Saturn rectification required for 7 consecutive Saturdays
9. On Tuesdays: take one handful of black gram, rotate for 7 times over head - repeat it thrice and then donate to some low-caste person

Jalandhar Astrologer:

1. Short tempered
2. Very hard working
3. Earns enough money but can't save
4. Mechanical job - related to manufacturing of machinery and parts
5. Underwent operation due to stomach problem
6. Married life - once divorced, to be divorced again
7. Wear Coral in gold ring
8. Saturn rectification required

HAROLD SHIPMAN as Kevin Richardson

Birth: 14-01-1946 at 8-40 AM (ST), Nottingham, UK

Source: www.astrolreport.com
www.zodiacal.com
www.astrotheme.fr

Late Harold Frederick Shipman, a British doctor, is the most known serial killer in the history of medical profession. He was convicted on 15 sample charges in 2000 and sentenced to 15 consecutive life sentences. He was accused of killing about 215 patients but it's also assumed that he killed more than 400 patients.

Dr. Shipman hanged himself in his cell in 2004, without admitting or explaining his crimes. He left behind his widow and four children.

HOROSCOPIC ANALYSIS

Jammu Astrologer:

1. Fond of wine and women
2. Late marriage or no marriage
3. Partnership good, sole proprietorship not beneficial
4. Business: Iron, Cloth, Hotel, Gift shop
5. No success in politics
6. Mars rectification required

Jalandhar Astrologer:

1. Sun in ascendant: dominating personality
2. Rahu-Saturn in 6th House: conquers enemies
3. Well respected in society
4. Happiness from children
5. Malefic Mars: two to three marriages
6. Mars rectification necessary for happy married life
7. Golden period: March 2008 to September 2010

Mathura Astrologer:

1. Saturn in the House of Diseases with Rahu: prone to diseases
2. Tension with wife
3. Wife will have blood related diseases
4. During the sub-period of Jupiter in the main-period of Saturn i.e. from March 2008 to September 2010: time good for political success
5. *Bagla Mukhi Sadhna* recommended for higher political achievements

IMRAN KHAN as Abdul Rashid

Birth: 25-11-1952 at 6-45 AM, Lahore, Pakistan

Source: Jyotish Sagar - July 2006

Imran Khan is regarded as one of the best all-rounders the game of cricket has ever produced. He was one of the fastest bowlers of the world during the late 1970s and early 1980s, and in the later half of his career, one of the best batsmen in the Pakistan team. Khan played cricket for Pakistan between 1971 and 1992 and was the captain of the team when Pakistan won its maiden World Cup in 1992.

After retiring from cricket, Khan established a charitable cancer hospital, 'Shaukat Khanum Memorial Cancer Hospital & Research Centre,' in Lahore using donations. In 1996, Khan founded his own political party 'Pakistan Tehreek-e-Insaaf'. Khan got married in 1995 and has two sons but in 2004, he got divorced.

HOROSCOPIC ANALYSIS

Jammu Astrologer:

1. Good education
2. Rich - high government post or sound business
3. Religious minded
4. Good relations with parents but not so good with brothers
5. Sun-Mercury combination: good management skills
6. Two marriages: second marriage between 10 February and 20 September 2007
7. Less interaction with children
8. Bad times after 12 October 2006
9. Saturn main-period from 1971 to 1992: indulgence in useless/wrong activities
10. Recommended stone: Ruby

Delhi Astrologer:

1. Relations not good with brothers - they can even harm him

2. Venus not favorable: financial position disturbed
3. Mercury not good: poor in Mathematics
4. Should seek blessings from elders
5. Donate green cloth at *Peer Baba* shrine
6. Prefer wearing white clothes
7. Good times ahead
8. Ruby and Emerald recommended
9. Venus rectification required: for marital and financial benefits

Gokul Astrologer:

1. Sun in ascendant: angry by nature
2. Venus in 2nd House: causes financial losses
3. Family and social life normal
4. Diamond recommended
5. Venus rectification required
6. Worship bo-tree on Saturdays

JAYENDRA SARASWATHI as Gajendran Iyer

Birth: 18-07-1935 at 7-30 AM, Erulniki, TN, India

Source: Future Samachar - January 2005

Jayendra Saraswathi Swamigal is a former, 69th *Shankracharya* (pontiff) of Kanchi Kamakoti Peetham (a prominent Hindu religious institution in Tamil Nadu) which was established by Adi Sankara in 482 B.C.E. and has the distinction of an un-broken lineage of 70 *Shankracharyas* till date.

Saraswathi was instrumental in establishing many educational institutions and hospitals to cater to the needs of the poor and needy. He also worked hard for the cause of removal of caste based differences in Hindu society and the ritual of animal sacrifice in temples.

In 2004, Jayendra Saraswathi remained in the headlines of national media because of his arrest on the charges of conspiring in the murder of a temple manager, Sankararaman. In January 2005, the Supereme Court of India granted him bail, after finding that there was no prima facie case made out against him. Jayendra Saraswathi is a *brahamchari* (never married).

HOROSCOPIC ANALYSIS

Jammu Astrologer:

1. Health-wise very inauspicious time until September 2007
2. Liver and heart weak, spinal cord mal-functioning
3. Struggling life, no success in anything
4. Troublesome married life but no divorce
5. Less interaction with siblings

Delhi Astrologer:

1. Egoistic and emotional
2. Uses rough language
3. Political success possible

4. Health problems for the last two and a half years- relief by April 2007
5. Mars-Jupiter together: less interaction with son
6. Yellow Sapphire in silver ring

Gokul Astrologer:

1. Normal nature
2. Reputation not good in society
3. Wife's health not good - Jupiter rectification needed
4. Children will not get share in his property: if children want property, they should perform *Nav-Graha Shanti havan*

LEONARDO DICAPRIO as Jason Alexander

Birth: 11-11-1974 at 2-47 AM (ST), Los Angeles, USA

Source: www.khaldea.com
www.zodiacal.com
www.astroprofile.com

Leonardo DiCaprio is an American actor who rose to international fame after the release of his film 'Titanic' (1997- the highest grossing movie ever worldwide). Suddenly, he became a household name, synonymous with labels such as 'teenage heartthrob' and 'sex symbol'. E! Online described him as the most gorgeous celebrity on the planet. His co-star Kate Winslet said that she agreed with others in deeming him the "most beautiful man on Earth".

Unfortunately for DiCaprio, his parents got divorced when he was just one year old. DiCaprio started his acting career at the age of 15 and has done wonderful work in many films since then. He is considered as one of the top stars and the most eligible bachelor in Hollywood.

HOROSCOPIC ANALYSIS

Jammu Astrologer:

1. Should be cautious about physical wellness
2. Sub-period of Jupiter in main-period of Mercury till December 2008 - big financial gains
3. Avoid alcohol and non-vegetarian food for success in films
4. Success in films between January and May 2008
5. Malefic Sun needs correction
6. Perform *Kartik shanti havan*
7. Wear *Lahsunia*

Delhi Astrologer:

1. Very ambitious
2. Jupiter strong, Sun and Moon weak

3. Overall struggling life
4. Bad time started from 2002 - big financial losses
5. Good time from December 2008 after the age of 35
6. Should prefer private job
7. Ruby recommended

Ludhiana Astrologer:

1. Good nature
2. Many hurdles in life - possibility of a law-suit soon
3. Business regarding Iron, Property, Petrol Pump (Gas Station) profitable
4. Success in politics is possible
5. Weakness in sex-power with passage of time
6. Two marriages, good number of children
7. Emerald recommended in gold ring
8. Sun worship required

MADONNA as Beverly Aadland

Birth: 16-08-1958 at 7-05 AM (ST), Bay City, Michigan, USA

Source: www.astrolreport.com
www.zodiacal.com
www.astrologysoftware.com

Madonna is the most known American female pop singer/ actress. She is the highest earning female singer of all times according to both the 2007 Guinness Book of Records and Billboard Magazine. In addition, Madonna holds the record for the top-grossing concert tour by a female artist.

Madonna's first marriage lasted from 1985 to 1989. In 1996, she gave birth to a daughter by her personal trainer but the couple ended their relationship in 1997. In 2000, she married again and had one son but it is reported that the couple is now seeking divorce and has been granted a preliminary 'quickie' divorce. She also has one adopted son.

HOROSCOPIC ANALYSIS

Jammu Astrologer:

1. Good relationship with mother
2. Eyes and head related diseases
3. Struggling life
4. Early marriage
5. Good administrator - Gift House, Readymade Garments business profitable
6. October 2005 to October 2008 - sub-period of Venus in main-period of Rahu: physical ailments, *Maha Lakshmi* worship recommended
7. Sun worship also required

Ludhiana Astrologer:

1. High degree in education - should be a Doctor

2. Settlement outside own country
3. Not-so-good relation with parents
4. Throat and stomach problems
5. Marriage after the age of 25 - married life good
6. Only one child
7. No scope in Music but will have interest in it

Jalandhar Astrologer:

1. Incomplete education
2. Gift Shop, Readymade Garments, Cosmetics business good for prosperity
3. Change of country possible
4. Professional success not very good
5. Good married life - only one husband
6. Rahu rectification required
7. Recommended - Diamond ring

MANOJ NIGHT SHYAMALAN as Piyush Arora

Birth: 06-08-1970 at 12-44 PM, Pondicherry, India

Source: www.astrolreport.com
www.astrotheme.fr
www.astrologysoftware.com

Manoj Night Shyamalan is an American writer and director (of Indian origin) who came to limelight after the mega success of his film 'The Sixth Sense'.

Shyamalan was born in India but just after six weeks of his birth, his parents moved to USA and he was raised there. He has written, produced and directed many blockbuster films and enjoys a very powerful position in American film industry. He became the highest paid screenwriter in Hollywood when Disney paid him $5 million to write their feature film 'Signs'. Shyamalan got married in 1993 and has two daughters.

HOROSCOPIC ANALYSIS

Jammu Astrologer:

1. Jupiter in ascendant: should be very intelligent
2. Rahu-period from 1990 to 2008: bad phase of life
3. Property related business good
4. Not willing for marriage yet (as of 2007)
5. Sub-period of Saturn in main-period of Rahu from January 1993 to June 2006: foreign travels went useless, wasted money
6. Good times after 2008
7. Recommended: Blue Sapphire

Ludhiana Astrologer:

1. Uses bad language and is cunning by nature
2. Earnings through illegal ways
3. Listens only to his heart

4. Playboy nature
5. If needed, he can be brought back to India and made a good human being through the power of *'siddhi'* (super-natural power)

Mathura Astrologer:

1. Fair complexioned and has good features
2. Blood pressure, acidity and stomach problems
3. Service line at clerical level in Police department
4. Less income, more expenditure
5. Family financial status good
6. Good with mother but not-so-good with father
7. Hindrance in education
8. Wife is bad tempered
9. Birth of children delayed due to wife's miscarriages/abortions
10. Minimum one son

PRIYANKA GANDHI as Neeta Kumari

Birth: 12-01-1972 at 2-40 PM, New Delhi, India

Source: www.astrodaily.com

Priyanka Gandhi (Vadra, surname after marriage) is the daughter, granddaughter, and great-granddaughter of Indian Prime Ministers. Her grandmother, late Mrs. Indira Gandhi and her father, late Mr. Rajiv Gandhi were brutally assassinated by some bad elements of their own country. Her mother, Mrs. Sonia Gandhi, now heads the Indian National Congress as its President and is the Chairperson of the United Progressive Alliance.

Priyanka is often compared to her charismatic grandmother and is fantasized by many Congress leaders to take her place. And though the Congress Party would love to hear her announcement to join active politics, Priyanka herself has not made any commitment as yet and prefers to strengthen the party without any portfolio. Her reluctance can be attributed to the brutal assassination of her father and grandmother. She is married and has two children.

HOROSCOPIC ANALYSIS

Jammu Astrologer:

1. Good education
2. Computer institute related business profitable
3. Below average social standing
4. Un-married: marriage possible from January 2007 to April 2008

Ludhiana Astrologer:

1. Struggling life
2. Within two years of her birth, more problems for her father
3. Incomplete education
4. Malefic Moon in 7th House: always problems with spouse
5. Less understanding with brothers

6. Arranged marriage
7. Before April 2007, loss of father or father-in-law and health problems for herself
8. Always in depression
9. Easy prone to cough and cold
10. Wear Pearl in silver locket
11. Wear Yellow Sapphire in first finger of left hand
12. Feed cows for five consecutive Wednesdays
13. Worship bo-tree on Saturdays
14. Avoid blue/black color painting in bedroom
15. No mirror and no religious photograph in bedroom
16. Keep one glass of water at bedside at night and in the morning, use the same water for watering the plants

Mathura Astrologer:

1. Long life
2. Saturn in ascendant giving full glance to the 7th House where Moon is malefic: not good for marriage
3. Should get married by July 2007
4. Husband not cooperative
5. Average life standard

RAHUL GANDHI as Yogesh Mishra

Birth: 19-06-1970 at 5-50 AM, New Delhi, India

Source: www.dayafterindia.com
www.astrodaily.com

Rahul Gandhi (Priyanka Gandhi's brother) is the son, grandson, and great-grandson of Indian Prime Ministers. His grandmother, late Mrs. Indira Gandhi and his father, late Mr. Rajiv Gandhi were brutally assassinated by some bad elements of their own country. His mother, Mrs. Sonia Gandhi, now heads the Indian National Congress as its President and is the Chairperson of the United Progressive Alliance.

Widely expected to join politics at an earlier age, Rahul, somehow, kept everybody anticipating regarding his decision. He fought the 2004 elections and was overwhelmingly elected Member of Parliament. His campaign was directed by his younger sister, Mrs. Priyanka Gandhi Vadra. In May 2009, he was again elected as Member of Parliament. It is widely speculated that Mrs. Sonia Gandhi is grooming him to become the next Prime Minister of India.

HOROSCOPIC ANALYSIS

Jammu Astrologer:

1. Good education
2. *Risht Yog*: keeping him un-married
3. Better not to get married
4. Professions related to education: School, College offering courses in Legal Studies, Politics, etc
5. Trading line not successful
6. Social status not very good

Ludhiana Astrologer:

1. *Mangalic*: chances of broken marriage if married before the age of 28

2. Marriage at the age of 32 years - has one boy, will have one girl too
3. Business prosperity if the business is in wife's name
4. Earned money but gone to drains
5. Normal success up to the age of 36 years
6. Influential just like his grandfather by the age of 22 years
7. *Raj Yog* : if prefers service line
8. Foreign travel/temporary settlement after March 2007

Delhi Astrologer:

1. Saturn and Moon malefic
2. *Mangalic*
3. Life full of struggle
4. Differences with father and brother
5. Long life
6. Property, Computer, Administration, Defense line related professions
7. Avoid partnerships
8. Intelligent but hindrances in education
9. Problems in married life
10. Never wear Blue Sapphire
11. Recommended: Emerald, White Sapphire
12. Moon main-period from 2007 to 2017: business and health problems, loss of reputation
13. Moon rectification and worship on Mondays
14. Saturn rectification also required

RAHUL DRAVID as Dushyant Chopra

Birth: 11-01-1973 at 11-00 AM, Indore, India

Source: www.astrodaily.com
www.navneetastrologer.com

Rahul Dravid is an Indian cricketer and former captain of the Indian cricket team. Rahul started his international cricket career in 1996 and as of December 2009, in terms of runs scored, he remains at number 4 position in Test cricket and number 6 position in One Day International cricket. He has more than 10000 runs to his name in both forms of the game. He is the fastest cricketer in the world to reach 9000 runs in Test cricket and the 1st Indian to score 5 double hundreds in Test cricket, each bigger than the previous one. He is also known as 'the wall' for his solid batting techniques. Rahul got married in 2003 and has a son.

HOROSCOPIC ANALYSIS

Jammu Astrologer:

1. Good education
2. Good home and good wife
3. Marriage by February 2007 within 20 km area of his home
4. Financially sound - job in private sector relating to Electronics, Petroleum, Rubber, Marble industry
5. Normal relations with siblings
6. Struggling life without much achievement
7. Settlement away from home

Mathura Astrologer:

1. Import-export, Commission Agent type profession profitable
2. Overall business prospect not good - should try for service
3. Venus main-period from 1999 to 2019: bad time
4. Sub-period of Rahu under main-period of Venus from January 2007 to January 2010
5. Yellow Sapphire in little finger of right hand

Kurukshetra Astrologer:

1. Stomach related problems
2. Good understanding with wife and happiness from children
3. Success when stays away from home
4. Moon in ascendant: frightening dreams haunt him
5. Mechanical line
6. No scope in Sports
7. Venus-period from 1999 to 2019: bad time
8. *Pitra-Dosh*: feed the cows and worship *Ganesha* (Hindu God)
9. Venus rectification: *Japa, Havan* required
10. Donations to be given at the time of Solar-eclipse
11. Coral and Pearl recommended

SACHIN TENDULKAR as Manish Saxena

Birth: 24-04-1973 at 4-25 PM, Mumbai, India

Source: Soubhagya Deep - July 2006
www.eastrovedica.com
www.astrodaily.com

Sachin Tendulkar is an Indian cricketer who is considered as one of the best batsmen the world has ever seen. He was rated by Wisden (2002) as the second greatest Test batsman after Sir Don Bradman. Sachin made his international debut in 1989 and as of December 2009, he remains the highest run scorer in Test cricket (12970 runs) as well as in One Day International cricket (17168 runs). Moreover, he also holds the record for maximum number of 100's in both forms of the game - 43 in Tests and 45 in ODIs.

Besides batting, Sachin is a part time bowler too and is fondly called as the man with a 'golden arm' who breaks partnerships. Sachin married at very young age of 22 and has one daughter and one son.

HOROSCOPIC ANALYSIS

Jammu Astrologer:

1. In-auspicious Rahu period - 1996 to 2014
2. *Kaal Sarp Dosh*
3. Mostly all Stars are unfavorable
4. Un-successful and un-married
5. Make offering of coconut and charcoal to the sea for three consecutive Saturdays
6. Donate two silver-snakes to a temple and make offering of two silver-snakes to the sea
7. Recite *Hanuman Chalisa Paath* (hymns related to God *Hanuman*) on Saturdays
8. Chant '*Om Shri Ganeshay Namaha*' for half an hour daily

Delhi Astrologer:

1. Should be a great saint with many spiritual powers
2. Astrologer/Computer Engineer/Businessman
3. No success in Sports because Mars is in 5th House with Jupiter
4. Paternal property dispute: property distribution in the next two and a half years, loss of personal savings
5. Settlement away from home
6. Good wife but she is not sexually satisfied
7. *Kaal Sarp Yog* - problems in financial matters (Mars-Saturn aspect)
8. 28-10-2006 to 16-11-2014: problems in married life and financial matters
9. Every year following his birthday: donate blankets, make offering to the sea of 4 dry coconuts and 4 Kg lead (single piece)
10. Do not eat fish, rather feed them
11. Wear *Lahsunia* in silver-ring on Thursday evening after sunset
12. Success in life after 2014

Gokul Astrologer:

1. Lord of ascendant in malefic Sign
2. *Paash Yog*
3. Betrayal from friends
4. Success through hard work only
5. *Kaal Sarp Yog*: unfavorable
6. Rahu in 4th House: in-auspicious
7. Delay in marriage or problems in married life
8. Mercury is malefic: disturbances in family life, wife is dominating
9. Sun in 8th House: prone to accidents
10. No success in Sports - Art related work profitable
11. *Kaal Sarp Yog* needs rectification

SATHYA SAI BABA as Kishan Lal

Birth: 23-11-1926 at 6-30 AM, Ananthapur, AP, India

Source: www.zodiacal.com
www.khaldea.com
www.astropro.com

Sathya Sai Baba is an Indian Hindu religious guru (preacher) and is famous all over the world for his image of a God-man and miracle worker. He is a *Brahamchari* (never married). According to the Sathya Sai Organization, there are an estimated 1,200 Sathya Sai Baba Centers in 130 countries world-wide.

Sathya Sai Baba's followers often report of his numerous incredible miracles: materializing substances from his hand such as *vibuthi* (holy ash), rings, watches, etc., levitation, healings, physical disappearances, physically transforming into various deities and physically emitting brilliant light, etc - the list is endless.

Moreover, in devotees' houses all around the world, it is reported that *vibhuti*, turmeric powder, holy water, sugar candy, fruits, herbs, *amrita* (nectar-like honey), writings in ash and various other substances spontaneously manifest and materialize on the walls, furniture, pictures and altars of Sathya Sai Baba.

While Baba has millions of devotees who vouch for him, there are also many critics who accuse him of being a 'skilled magician' without any so-called divine powers.

HOROSCOPIC ANALYSIS

Jammu Astrologer:

1. Problematic relations with wife
2. Sun-Saturn together in ascendant: problems with sons
3. Breathing problems to continue
4. November 1999 to January 2003 - sub-period of Saturn under main-period of Venus : death either of spouse or his own

5. *Maha Mrityunjya japa* required - avoid onion and garlic
6. Use silver glass for drinking water or milk
7. Recommended: wear *Gomed* in *Panchdhatu* (mixture of five metals: copper, gold, lead, silver and iron) locket

Kurukshetra Astrologer:

1. Venus-Mercury in ascendant and Jupiter in 3rd House aspect 7th House : two marriages
2. Moon-Rahu in 8th House: problematic
3. 1999 to 2007: health problems
4. Rahu rectification required
5. Feed the beggars on Wednesdays and grass to cows on every New Moon

Jalandhar Astrologer:

1. Government job
2. Very adamant
3. Religious minded but doesn't do it from heart
4. Loves: wine, women and non-vegetarian food
5. Physical problem for the last six months - unknown disease, stomach and joint pains
6. Has marks on face

SALMAN RUSHDIE as Ataullah Khan

Birth: 19-06-1947 at 2-25 AM, Mumbai, India

Source: www.astrolreport.com
www.astropro.com
www.astrotheme.fr

Sir Ahmed Salman Rushdie is an Indian author who suddenly came to limelight after Mr. Ayatollah Khomeini (then Supreme leader of Iran) issued a *fatwa* (religious edict) for Rushdie's death for having written 'The Satanic Verses' (in 1988). As a result of *fatwa* and threats from Muslim world, Rushdie remained underground for most of the period in the following decade.

Rushdie's second novel, 'Midnight's Children' (1981), won him the prestigious Booker Prize. In 1993, the award was judged to have been the 'Booker of Bookers', the best novel to have won the Booker Prize for fiction in the award's 25-year history. In July 2008, 'Midnight's Children' won a public vote to be named the Best of the Booker, the best novel to win the Booker Prize in the award's 40-year history. Rushdie was awarded British Knighthood in the 2007 Queen Elizabeth's Birthday Honors for his services to literature. Rushdie has married four times but all his marriages have ended in divorce. He has two children.

HOROSCOPIC ANALYSIS

Jammu Astrologer:

1. Professional life is good
2. Relations not good with wife, may have died
3. Should have a mistress
4. Last six and a half years very bad, conditions will improve after July 2007
5. Bad relations with father and son
6. Will inherit all paternal wealth, won't share with siblings
7. Better to stay away from son

8. Over indulgence in women and wine would be the cause of his death
9. Bad reputation in society
10. Recommended stone: Coral

Delhi Astrologer:

1. Computer, Accounts, Travelling related occupation
2. More than one occupation, good income
3. Income from illegal ways - monetary benefits also from wife
4. Good health and strong mental power
5. Better to remain away from home otherwise problems with family members
6. Satisfaction from children
7. Less friends
8. Not very cordial relations with wife
9. Business problems since 20-3-2002 but even then things will remain satisfactory
10. Feed black dogs and beggars
11. Donate yellow cloth to a Mosque/Temple on Thursday for once or twice every year
12. Wear Ruby in gold ring on Sunday
13. Avoid the numbers whose sum totals to 8

Kurukshetra Astrologer:

1. Good education
2. Occupation: Engineering, Astrology, Temple services related
3. Married life upset but happiness from children
4. Health not very good - sex related diseases, skin allergy
5. Homely atmosphere not very good
6. Problems since 2004 - may go under depression very soon
7. Mercury and Jupiter rectification required

SHILPA SHETTY as Anita Shrivastav

Birth: 08-06-1975 at 7-00 PM, Mumbai, India

Source: Jyotish Sagar - January 2006

Shilpa Shetty is an Indian Film actress who has worked in more than 50 films (Hindi, Tamil, Telugu and Kannada) since making her debut in 1993.

In January 2007, Shilpa came to international limelight not because of some film but because of her emerging as winner of the British TV show 'Celebrity Big Brother'. The controversial show became a worldwide hit because of the alleged racial abuse of Shilpa by the other housemates of the show. Shilpa is married and working on many projects.

HOROSCOPIC ANALYSIS

Jammu Astrologer:

1. No success in life before the age of 34
2. Marriage after June 2007
3. Love marriage in a different caste
4. Any money, if earned at all, will go waste
5. Professional or otherwise settlement in life after the age of 34
6. Wear *Zarkan* in the index finger of left hand

Delhi Astrologer:

1. Good education
2. Stomach problems
3. 2002 to 2006 - bad time: health problems and financial losses
4. Marriage in 2008: misunderstandings with husband
5. Good time after April 2007
6. No success in Film line
7. *Kalankit Yog*: untimely death
8. Recommended: *Sarv Vijay* worship

Gokul Astrologer:

1. Good education, good earnings but less savings
2. No control over emotions - betrayal from lover would earn her bad name
3. Very moody and determined
4. *Budhaditya Raj Yog*: success after marriage
5. Lord of the 10th House is in *Grahan Yog*: will not get what she wants, so no chance in Films as an actress
6. Interior decoration, Boutique or Art related business profitable
7. *Manglik Yog*: delay in marriage
8. Marriage in 2007 in West direction
9. Should be careful about eye diseases
10. Rahu rectification required

TIMMOTHY MCVEIGH as Rick Springfield

Birth: 23-04-1968 at 8-30 AM (ST), Lockpot, New York, USA

Source: www.astrolreport.com
www.zodiacal.com
www.astrotheme.fr

Late Timmothy James McVeigh was the man behind the bombing of Alfred P. Murrah federal building in Oklahoma City (USA) in 1995 and is commonly referred to as the Oklahoma City bomber. The bombing was the deadliest incident of terrorism in the U.S. history until the 9/11 (2001) attack on the World Trade Center in New York. McVeigh was executed by lethal injection in 2001.

McVeigh was a decorated U.S. Army veteran who worked in the Gulf War from 1988 to 1991(he was awarded a Bronze star). In a book, 'American Terrorist', based on interviews before his execution, McVeigh stated that (during Gulf war) he was shocked to be ordered to execute surrendering prisoners and to see carnage on the road leaving Kuwait City after U.S. troops routed the Iraqi army. McVeigh said he began harboring anti-government feelings during the Gulf War.

Moreover, after returning from the war, there were still many U.S. government policies that kept on offending him every now and then. While in jail, he regretted that so many innocent people had died because of the bombing - he claimed that his motto was not to kill the innocent people but only to teach the govt. a lesson.

HOROSCOPIC ANALYSIS

Jammu Astrologer:

1. Daring and hard working
2. Very social - good with everybody
3. Partnership beneficial
4. Good scope in politics
5. Electronic work profitable
6. Marriage after October 2007: married life good

Delhi Astrologer:

1. Good nature and helpful
2. People generally cheat him
3. Sun is powerful: will-power strong
4. Less struggle in life
5. Good period after October 2007
6. Overall favorable Stars: major achievement in next 7 years
7. Suggested stones: Emerald and Blue Sapphire

Gokul Astrologer:

1. Medicine, Chemicals, Minerals, Health Equipment related business profitable
2. *Gaj Kesari* and *Budhadhi Yog*: success in politics possible
3. Hard working but less successful
4. *Kaal Sarp Yog* and Saturn-Rahu *Yog*: hindrance in overall achievement in life
5. Saturn aspect 7th House: two marriages possible
6. Second marriage possible after November 2007
7. Good reputation in society because of two *Raj Yog*
8. *Kaal Sarp Yog*: rectification required

PRINCE WILLIAM as George Smith

Birth: 21-06-1982 at 9-03 PM (DST), Paddington, UK

Source: www.astrolreport.com
www.zodiacal.com
www.astroprofile.com

Prince William is the elder son of Prince Charles (Prince of Wales) and late Diana (Princess of Wales). He is second in line to the British throne.

Prince William is a commissioned officer in the British Army. He is Patron or President to a small number of organizations whose work he wants to support. He is also a keen sportsman and enjoys a variety of activities, mostly team sports.

HOROSCOPIC ANALYSIS

Jammu Astrologer:

1. Should be working in technical field and should not change job till one and a half year
2. Will marry at his birth place
3. Has some strong fear and insecurity inside
4. Marriage should be in 2008
5. Yellow Sapphire recommended

Ludhiana Astrologer:

1. Should start his own business before May 2008
2. Marriage according to family wishes
3. Less interaction with father
4. Less happiness from mother
5. Will listen more to outsiders
6. Will have two marriages in life
7. Overall life is good

Delhi Astrologer:

1. Ketu in ascendant is not favorable: problematic to others
2. Overall not good in education but very good in Mathematics
3. Computer related work good for business
4. Mercury and Venus favorable: many benefits in life especially in money matters
5. Normal problems in married life
6. Good relations with parents
7. Overall analysis: 60% un-favorable Stars
8. Recommended stones: Pearl and Yellow Sapphire
9. Should wear yellow dresses more
10. Rectification required for - Mercury, Jupiter and Rahu

HOROSCOPIC ANALYSIS OF NON-CELEBRITY TEST SUBJECTS

So, that's how astrologers from different parts of India interpreted the horoscopes of these celebrities! You can very well judge the validity of astrology from these readings. All the readings have been somewhat of general nature. No astrologer could tell from the horoscopes of George Bush or Sachin Tendulkar or Madonna or Sathya Sai Baba or Prince Charles - about their international fame, achievements and other important factors associated with their life. But, if only they were told about the names of the real subjects, they would have surely described those auspicious astrological combinations that made them so great!

Well, that's the real truth about this centuries-old superstition. Now, let's see how astrologers interpreted horoscopes of the people whom I personally know. I have no doubt about the birth date and time of these individuals. The names of the test subjects have been changed for the sake of their privacy. A brief description about the life of the subjects would be given before readings made by the astrologers.

NAVEEN KAPOOR

Birth: 30-09-1968 at 2-30 AM, Jammu, India

Number three of four sons of very down to earth and gentle parents, Naveen chose to live a not-so-gentle life. While his elder brothers were pursuing studies and helping in family business, Naveen made friendship with the local underworld mafia. Soon, he earned good reputation in his field while his family had to undergo a lot of humiliation and police torture because of his crimes. Nonetheless, Naveen's reputation and contacts in the mafia world did help his brothers to achieve phenomenal success in their new business as govt. contractors. After years of hide-and-seek game with the police department, Naveen finally decided to live a gentle life and has now settled most of his pending cases. Today he lives a happy married and rather peaceful life with his wife and two sons.

HOROSCOPIC ANALYSIS

Jammu Astrologer:

1. Mars and Jupiter together in Cancer ascendant: education is very good
2. Marriage Yog between 2003 to 2006 but Saturn together with Rahu is problematic
3. Marriage very much possible in 2008
4. Should have good number of children
5. Jupiter period starts from 2016 onwards - especially good for wealth
6. Despite government job, he can also do private business especially Contractual works
7. Yellow Sapphire and Coral are lucky stones
8. Should donate goods related to Saturn and Rahu
9. Should worship Sun

Jalandhar Astrologer:

1. Planets placed strongly in the horoscope
2. Has good status in society

3. Will earn good money in life using his brain power
4. Should perform Sun and Ketu worship
5. Should wear Blue Sapphire

Delhi Astrologer:

1. Education should be up to degree level
2. Job should be computer related in Police or Army
3. Married life should be normal
4. Until mid 2007 - shortage of money and health problems for wife
5. Should have own double storey house
6. Wear Pearl and Coral in silver rings

ARVIND TRIPATHI

Birth: 10-07-1965 at 5-00 AM, Jammu, India

Middle son of three sons of a business class family, Arvind had to play the Godfather after his father died untimely. He managed the family business while supporting his elder brother in completing his engineering degree and younger brother his graduation. Everything went fine again; Arvind got married in time and had two sons. But when it came to the settlement of family wealth, he was not very satisfied with his share. He believed that he deserved more and remained upset for some years. Anyhow, things became normal with time. Eight years back, when he felt some pain in the chest and went to hospital for general check-up, doctors declared that he had heart problem and an open-heart surgery was performed. Arvind now lives a normal happy married life.

HOROSCOPIC ANALYSIS

Jammu Astrologer:

1. Should be an industrialist
2. Take precaution in partnerships
3. 2nd marriage possible in 2008
4. First wife died because of sickness
5. Should be suffering from urinal infections
6. Cloth business is also beneficial
7. Sun creating problems in married and business life
8. Ruby and Sun-Yantra recommended
9. Worship god *Vishnu*

Ludhiana Astrologer:

1. Can have severe physical ailment from January 2007 to May 2007
2. Has the tendency to waste money
3. There should be a young death in his family
4. An elder in his family should be on bed for the last two years
5. No chance for settlement abroad

6. Should perform Saturn worship
7. *Kaal Sarp Yog* is strong - perform *Maha Mrityunjya Jaap*

Delhi Astrologer:

1. Religious but disturbed in life
2. No paternal wealth and no savings
3. Towering personality but without any impact
4. Angry by nature, egoistic
5. Friends not favorable
6. Delay in marriage or no marriage; if married, should not be happy
7. Profession requires lot of hard work
8. Financial gains very difficult
9. Should avoid use of number 8
10. Should wear Emerald in gold ring
11. Should worship lord *Hanuman*
12. Should worship Sun daily

AVINASH KHANNA

Birth: 05-11-1960 at 9-18 AM, Jammu, India

Avinash got into his family business when he was just studying at college. Because of the early death of his mother, he was married at young age of 23. He has two sons and one daughter. He is hard working, introvert and miser by nature. He is one of the leading businessmen of his line in the city. One can say that he has lived an overall good life till date - no financial, family or health problems.

HOROSCOPIC ANALYSIS

Jammu Astrologer:

1. Health related problems to remain till the age of 52
2. Private job better than own business
3. 50th year of life especially good
4. Lucky numbers are 4, 5 and 6
5. Problems in married life due to the wrong direction of the gate of the house - shift the gate from East to South. South is the only suitable and lucky direction for this person
6. Malefic Sun needs correction for better health
7. Should worship Sun daily
8. Coral and Ruby are essential stones

Mathura Astrologer:

1. Long struggle for settlement in life - success after changing three businesses
2. Sun aspects the House of Income and moreover Rahu is in that House - not good for business
3. Dispute with brothers - less share in parental property
4. The House of Wife in the chart is not auspicious - unhappiness in relationship with wife
5. Recommended stone: *Gomed*
6. Serve fruit to beggars on Wednesdays

7. Distribute sweets to children after making offerings to Lord *Hanuman* on Saturdays

Delhi Astrologer:

1. Sun is malefic: bad period to remain from December 2006 until September 2007
2. Many upsets in life until 2012
3. Trouble in family life - separation from wife possible
4. Tension can even cause brain hemorrhage

DEEPIKA RAZDAN

Birth: 08-09-1978 at 2-50 AM, Jammu, India

Born in a middle class family, while pursuing her studies, Deepika fell in love with a neighborhood boy and wanted to marry him. Initially, there was some disagreement about the boy, but ultimately her parents yielded to her request. Deepika's horoscope correctly matched with that of the boy and they were married. Everything in their marriage went fine and soon they had a daughter. But, the boy's addictive habits, previously ignored, had now increased to such an extent that he had to be, ultimately, admitted into a de-addiction centre where he committed suicide (as per reports). Deepika remained widow for four years but in 2008, she was re-married to a widower with one son. She is a housewife and lives a happy life now with her daughter, her husband and his son. Deepika has an elder married sister and a younger un-married brother.

HOROSCOPIC ANALYSIS

Jammu Astrologer:

1. Should be working in some technical field
2. Will go abroad for job before May 2008
3. Will marry an NRI after May 2008 and settle abroad
4. Husband will progress more after marriage
5. Husband should also be in technical field
6. Married life will be very good
7. Wear Pearl in silver ring
8. Should feed dogs daily
9. Don't eat/drink food (of white color) at night, drink milk in the morning

Ludhiana Astrologer:

1. Good education and good nature
2. Good husband, beautiful home, luxury vehicles
3. More chances for government service and should also marry service class

4. If she had sex before marriage, effects of all planets will change for worse
5. Should pray to the Goddess for forgiveness
6. Wear Diamond in gold ring
7. Perform *Kaal Sarp* worship

Delhi Astrologer:

1. Sun placed well in the horoscope - financially good
2. Wear Coral for rectifying weak Mars
3. Jupiter well placed - good savings
4. Growth in Teaching profession
5. Should do important works on Tuesdays
6. Married life will be good - husband will be a professional
7. Marriage outside state or country better

MADHURI WALIA

Birth: 27-01-1973 at 2-15 AM, Jammu, India

At the age of 35, Madhuri is now a divorcee with a 9 year old son. Born in a reputed family of educated parents and grandparents, she was educated in a Convent school. Thereafter, she obtained her degree in Electronics Engineering from Mumbai. After two years of marriage and the birth of a boy, differences with husband started growing. Then, the couple got separated and finally divorced after eight years of their marriage. Among other misfortunes, Madhuri never got a job in her own field and had to compromise with odd jobs. She now lives in her parental home (mother expired when she was un-married) and is the head of an educational institute. Madhuri has two married sisters and one un-married brother.

HOROSCOPIC ANALYSIS

Jammu Astrologer:

1. Adamant nature, barely obeys others
2. Problems in education
3. Her mother should be short-tempered
4. Should have three brothers
5. New house before 28 years of age
6. Marriage not favorable until 34 years of age
7. Will suffer from chest pain and cold
8. Suggested stones - Ruby, Emerald and Iron ring

Mathura Astrologer:

1. Good education and reputation
2. Married life not satisfactory
3. Relationship with in-laws not very cordial
4. Husband's business better after marriage
5. One child and one miscarriage
6. Should worship lord *Shiva* and feed the birds

Jalandhar Astrologer:

1. Cool nature because of Moon's position in the chart
2. Can get problems in life because of a 3rd person
3. Property business good for profession
4. Overall good married life
5. Should make donations on Saturdays and do Saturn worship
6. Should feed wheat to the fish or cows for lessening bad effects of Rahu and Ketu
7. Should worship Mars

MAHESH KUMAR

Birth: 01-05-1958 at 7-10 AM, Jammu, India

Being the youngest in family and born after the birth of three sisters, Mahesh got full attention and affection of his parents. Intelligent right from his school days, Mahesh completed his P.G. in Business Management and wanted to join some multi-national company. But, out of compulsion, he had to join his father's business. His life has been quite normal so far - no major physical or financial problems. He lives a happy married life with his wife and two adult children.

HOROSCOPIC ANALYSIS

Jammu Astrologer:

1. Should be in Teaching profession
2. Un-happy with respect to progeny: has only female children
3. Can have heart related problems in 2007
4. Dispute with brothers regarding family property
5. Litigation will tarnish his image in the society and there would be loss of money as well
6. Should avoid alcohol to gain success in litigation
7. Ruby and Pearl are recommended
8. Should worship lord *Vishnu*

Delhi Astrologer:

1. Should be suffering from blood related disease for the last six months
2. Should get relief between January and July 2007
3. After July 2007, Saturn *Sadhe Sati* (very inauspicious period of Saturn) of two and a half years start - strong precautions to be taken
4. Business will yield profits after January 2007
5. Should have an elder sister who often remains sick
6. Will not have good relations with brothers
7. Should wear White Sapphire in silver ring

8. Should donate green clothes to children below the age of 8 years
9. Should make offerings to the river for three consecutive Wednesdays: 108 lead-Snakes, 108 Rahu *yantras*, 108 Fish *yantras*, 4 coconuts and a 4 kg piece of lead

Mathura Astrologer:

1. Enjoys well-established business
2. Has lost a very good chance of owning a big piece of land
3. Earns money but also suffers losses
4. Has good heart towards wife but still there are chances of divorce
5. Second marriage is possible
6. Should wear Coral

RITIKA VERMA

Birth: 03- 02-1961 at 3-40 AM, Jammu, India

Born in a family of four sisters and two brothers, Ritika wanted to go for higher studies. But before she could complete her studies, Ritika was married at a young age. Well, she managed to cope up with the situation and adjusted herself well in her in-laws house. Ritika never had any major problem in life and lives a happy married life with her husband and two children.

HOROSCOPIC ANALYSIS

Jammu Astrologer:

1. Should be suffering from acute illness since May 2006
2. Husband is not very cooperative and ill-treats her
3. Financial problems to remain until September 2008
4. Got higher education but preferred to be housewife
5. Problems with in-laws especially sister-in-law to remain
6. Lucky number is 7
7. Observe fast on Mondays and worship lord *Shiva*
8. Donate black blankets to beggars for three consecutive Saturdays following her birthday

Delhi Astrologer:

1. Has very quarrelsome nature since childhood
2. Good professional but bad housewife
3. *Yog* indicating that ill health may remain for a longer period than expected. Also, inauspicious for husband's health
4. Should feed the blinds
5. Wear a square-piece of gold in the neck
6. Donate one black and one white blanket to a temple
7. Make offering of milk to any sacred river on Mondays
8. Wear Yellow Sapphire in gold ring
9. Observe fast and worship lord *Shiva* on Mondays

Mathura Astrologer:

1. Average education
2. Miser by nature and also short tempered
3. Prone to accidents
4. Wheatish complexion, should have a prominent mark on face
5. Should have four sons
6. Wear Ruby

SHEFALI SAXENA

Birth: 13-12-1971 at 9-10 AM, Jammu, India

Shefali got married at the late age of 28 to an old friend whom she thought was compatible, after having turned down many proposals. After her marriage, she chose not to continue her business and handed it over to her younger sister. After marriage, she worked for three years in USA while her husband was pursuing his studies there. On returning back from USA, she gave birth to a baby girl after 6 years of marriage (by choice). Though she had all comforts in life, yet she remained upset for about five years because of her husband's decision to re-settle in USA. As of April 2009, Shefali enjoys a relaxed and happy life as her husband has now changed his mind.

HOROSCOPIC ANALYSIS

Jammu Astrologer:

1. Bad period until January 2007 - mental tension, anger, financial instability
2. Good education
3. Good relation with in-laws
4. Should have two kids
5. Initial and last period of life is good
6. Prone to eyes and throat related diseases
7. Recommended stone - Diamond
8. Should worship Sun

Delhi Astrologer:

1. Greedy for materialistic things in life
2. Sound parental property
3. Weak personality
4. Not happy with father and husband
5. No business or service
6. Less earnings

7. Should distribute yellow cloth to the poor in temples on her birthdays every year
8. Should feed green vegetables/grass to cows on Wednesdays
9. Should make offerings to Sun and chant *Gaytri Mantra* daily
10. Avoid numbers whose sum totals to 9

Rishikesh Astrologer:

1. Jupiter period of 16 years started from 1990 but Jupiter not strongly placed in 12th House - mental tension, physical problems, loss in authority but benefits in land and property
2. July 2004 to November 2006 - sub-period of Rahu in Jupiter main-period: not auspicious with regard to children, sour relations with siblings
3. Jupiter, lord of ascendant, in 12th House will help in settling abroad
4. Professional achievement in life will start after 2007
5. Many comforts in life but health matters always worrisome
6. Yellow Sapphire and Ruby recommended
7. Should worship Sun
8. Observe fasting on Thursdays and worship banana tree
9. Donate iron, black blanket, black cloth, etc.

VISHAL GANDOTRA

Birth: 20-02-1969 at 12-25 PM, Jammu, India

Hailing from a low middle class family and with education only up to under-graduate level, Vishal was lucky enough to get married (love) to an engineer girl from a high status family and had a son. But sadly, his relations with wife started to change for the worse. Then, they were separated and finally divorced. Now, after two years of divorce, Vishal is still un-married. Known for his ill-mannerisms and stubborn attitude, he still finds ways to torment his ex-wife.

HOROSCOPIC ANALYSIS

Jammu Astrologer:

1. Saturn not well placed, during Saturn periods: problems in family life, bad relations with parents, litigations, less income
2. *Mangalic* - wife should also be *Mangalic* otherwise tension in married life but still no chance of divorce
3. Three children
4. *Naag Yog* - mentally upset, hurdles in progress

Ludhiana Astrologer:

1. Betrayal in partnership with people of Virgo Sign
2. Good relation with brothers,normal relation with wife
3. Wear Yellow Sapphire in gold ring in index finger of right hand
4. Wear yellow clothes on Thursdays
5. Worship lord *Hanuman* and observe religious rituals for 40 days

Mathura Astrologer:

1. Own business good for progress
2. Good relations with brother but not so good relations with father
3. Married life will be normal

HOW AND WHY FORTUNE-TELLING SYSTEMS STILL EXIST!?

Well... well... well... So, you have yourself seen as to how the astrologers interpreted these horoscopes!

Though in this age, astrology should have been a thing of the past but shamefully, it still exists. The main reason behind its existence is the lack of awareness on the part of those who could really make a difference - the influential government heads and the bosses of print and electronic media. Moreover, there is an acute dearth of intellectuals and popular personalities (who can easily influence the masses) who really want to do something for the society. Everybody is living in their own selfish world where they are always looking for 'contacts' that can provide them more 'contracts'.

The ordinary people don't have time to get the awareness, essential for a better living in 21st century. After toiling and wondering over God's drama the whole day, they prefer to watch 'breaking news', 'dance numbers', 'comedy shows', etc. etc. If one had time to gain some knowledge about world history, evolution, religions, mythologies, scientific achievements, etc. - the world would have been a much better place today devoid of religious differences and superstitions.

All religions proclaim that Creation started from their homeland. Going by that theory, there should be at least 50 - 100 Gods. Now, is it possible that a child can have 100 fathers? Common sense tells us that there can only be one father. Now, everyone is trying to prove their God the real Creator! The broad-minded people with wide knowledge understand the truth. But, the percentage of such people is still very less. Even a government is formed by the majority votes and things sell well in the market if liked by the majority populace. Understanding this common formula, one can understand as to why astrology and other misleading superstitions are still prevalent in our society.

Well, I have this strong feeling that even the people who believe in astrology have a certain element of doubt in their minds. But, since their inner-most faith lies with astrology, they ignore its short-comings and like to justify their faith by remembering the predictions made by astrologers long time back: "*Panditji* (astrologer) had rightly predicted that I would become a doctor". OK, he has become a doctor but the doctor ignores many other things also predicted by the astrologer, such as at the age of 35 he's still a bachelor whereas *Panditji* had predicted that "By the age of 35, I'll be father of two kids". It's highly disgusting that many so-called well educated people of our society still believe in such superstitions. I myself have personally met many intellectuals who believe in absurd religious beliefs and superstitions. By the end of our discussions, they either get annoyed or just make excuse, finding it impossible to answer me.

Now, apart from lack of awareness, let's figure out as to how and why astrology still works:

Reason No. 1 :

A fortune-teller (astrologer, palmist, numerologist, tarot-card reader, psychic, etc) usually makes many predictions every day. Most of the times, people ask them questions, to which the fortune-teller answers. Now, it's just a matter of chance that some of the predictions would come true whereas most of them would not. During a fortune telling session, the believers themselves give enough clues to the fortune-tellers for validating their 'science'. Now, what happens after the session is that the believer only likes to remember the predictions that turned out to be true. And for those that didn't turn out true, the fortune-tellers still have many reasons for satisfying the faithful believers. Here, the problem is that people are made to believe that the Planet and Star Gods are the basic source of their miseries and that an astrologer is the only person who can really help them by pleasing these Gods.

Reason No. 2 :

I believe (on the basis of some personal experiences) that some astrologers attain certain kind of *siddhi* (ability to contact supernatural powers/higher spirit forms or some sort of psychic/ clairvoyant abilities) by which they can know the past and present events of your life and may also read your mind (well, if you are sure that there is no such power as *siddhi* and that I am misguided, kindly guide me). Now, they won't reveal their *siddhi* but rather pose as astrologers. If you happen to visit such an astrologer, the astrologer will pose to study your horoscope and start reading, "Ok, hum.. so you lost your mother at the age of 15... and since the last 4 years, you are having problems with your wife... you have a son... now you are worried about the litigation... hunh?". Aghast, all you would do is just nod!

But, their *siddhi* can reveal only this much. From there the astrologer takes over, he/she would now predict your future as per questions asked. Thereafter, you would be advised some remedies - donate certain things to certain type of people... wear certain colored clothes on certain days... wear certain stones... perform certain rituals, etc. etc. You would handsomely pay the astrologer and do whatever you were told. After all, you want to win the litigation and the astrologer has very rightly read your past and now under his/her directions, your future will be good. No person on earth can convince you now that astrology is fake. But again, the chances that the predictions would turn out to be true are the same as with the predictions made by the astrologer without the power of any *siddhi*. I have personally met a few astrologers who had attained *siddhi* and it was their influence that I initially believed in astrology. Later on, I befriended one of them and the secret was revealed to me.

Reason No. 3 :

Astrology works because of the centuries old belief that 'astrology works'. A distressed person needs some hope/miracle and the fulfillment of that hope is promised by the astrologers/occultists (*tantriks*). Nobody minds spending some money for the fulfillment of their dreams. Here, the law of probability applies - sometimes you succeed and sometimes you fail. But, the failure doesn't make you disbelieve astrology. Moreover, you don't have time to think about the validity of astrology. Soon... you move on with life. But, you again remember astrologers when you are in some problem. The cycle goes on like that... forever... and ever.

PRACTICAL SUGGESTIONS FOR ASTROLOGERS

One day astrology would be out of our minds but one would always wonder as to how it all started and would wholeheartedly appreciate the efforts made by the ancient astrologers in reading the skies. In an age, when there were no telescopes and high-tech labs, the ancient astrologers studied the skies with naked eyes for years together and documented their observations. You can very well understand their labor if you try to find out the positions of planets and stars with naked eyes.

Frankly speaking, I have tried it myself and can't help but salute the patience of the ancient astrologers in watching skies. Their observations did help the humankind know about different directions and the timing of different seasons. But, since astrology was mainly developed in Northern hemisphere, that knowledge was more useful for the people living in that half of the earth.

The humans have always been afraid of the wrath of the Gods and have been trying to figure out different ways to get their blessings. Living on planet Earth, it was very natural for them to think that the Sky Gods (astronomical bodies) were watching them and affecting their life. With that belief in mind, they studied the positions and movements of the astronomical bodies. If something good or bad occurred on a certain day and by chance a similar event occurred on the same day in the next cycle, an astrological formula was born. With the passage of time, hundreds and thousands of formulae were formulated, thus, forming basis for 'astrology'.

Astrologers can also be called the forefathers of 'astronomy'. Their knowledge about the positions and movements of Sky Gods helped humans in developing the science of astronomy.

Many a time, it has happened in the history that centuries-old myths have died their natural death. Ironically, many still exist and one of them is astrology. But how long can it exist? With more knowledge and awareness and the most important thing, when humans now have the courage to acknowledge 'truth', astrology and many such superstitions will also die their natural death. Can anyone still declare that:-

1. Earth is flat
2. All the planets and stars revolve around the earth
3. The divine grandma is spinning Charkha on the Moon
4. Earth is resting on the horns of the divine Ox
5. There is nothing beyond the ocean
6. Demons live on the other side of the mountain
7. Only the followers of a certain religion can enter Heaven (as once claimed in an election rally by Mr. George W. Bush, ex-President of USA - sadly there are still many superstitious people at such high levels)
8. Planet Earth was the first creation of God
9. The Creation came into being some ten thousand years back (Biblical accounts)
10. The human creation started from India or Iraq or Japan or Mexico, etc etc

The list is endless and one can easily come to the conclusion only if one is well-read and broad-minded. Sorrowfully, a very small percentage of the human population comes into that category. Many a time, people know the truth but prefer to go with the crowd for the fear of being 'left alone'. Anyhow, my point is that sooner or later, misleading and useless superstitions/myths will die their natural death.

Here, the astrologers need to understand the realities of the present world. They should first of all test the 'truth of astrology' themselves rather than believing in it fanatically and stop complimenting themselves as saviors of the humankind. Now, the problem is that the astrologers don't even want to discuss the validity of astrology. For them, it is the ultimate and un-questionable 'eternal truth' as described by the ancient *rishis* (religious scholars) in the sacred texts. Everything should happen according to the doctrines of astrology and if something didn't happen accordingly, there must be some 'divine intervention' over which no mortal has any control. Going by this 'divine intervention' theory, astrology can never be challenged. For astrologers, all the Planets and Stars are Gods and who can challenge

Gods if they choose to change their will? So, going by this philosophy, astrology is a vital part of religion. How can one challenge religion? If somebody dares, he/she should be prosecuted to death!

The astrologers have all the logic of the world to claim that astrology works. But, if asked, they cannot actually prove that astrology works. Though there are all sorts of astrological formulae that are claimed to predict future after the birth of a child. But, detailed researches undertaken over long periods of time all over the world have proved that astrology can't predict anything - even past and present events in the life of an individual, forget the future predictions. So practically there is no truth in astrology.

Now, astrologers need to understand that astrology can't survive for long in the present world. They need to get rid of pre-conceived notions. But the problem is that astrology is also connected with religion and mythology. By accepting that astrology does not work, many questions come into picture - many astrological Gods are worshipped and then even their existence can be challenged. But, going by common sense, the mythological gods of ancient civilizations don't really have any place in today's world. Thousands of years back, out of fear and devotion, human imagination created thousands of Gods all over the world. The people of India, Iraq, China, Japan, Greece, Egypt, Canada, Mexico, North Europe, etc. - all have mythological stories that Gods started Creation from their homeland. This theory could be believable in those times by the people living in those lands. But today it's totally un-acceptable. A child cannot have hundred fathers.

Now, some of the old rituals have already been banned by the government - say for example, human or animal sacrifice to please the Gods. Here, a useless, misleading and cruel cult has been abolished without undermining the dignity of the Gods to whom these sacrifices were made. Similarly, the misleading and useless 'fortune-telling' systems can also be banned by the government.

Agreed that the astrologers have devoted their whole life in learning astrology and earn their livelihood through this profession but now they will also have to take the initiative to test the validity of astrology. When they do so, they (the honest ones) would abandon their practice and start looking for some noble profession. Astrologers always claim to help people, well, there are many other ways to help people - they can form NGOs/Societies and obtain grants from the government. This way, they can draw suitable salaries for themselves and also help people when the need arises. They can utilize self-employment schemes of various government agencies. Their potential can also be utilized by the astronomy departments as they have good knowledge of the astronomical bodies, their position, their movements, etc. In short, there are many ways by which the astrologers can earn their livelihood. But, unfortunately, most of them have become used to living the life of a 'freeloader'.

Well, whatever the practising astrologers decide for themselves, no way should they guide their children into this profession as that would be the biggest blunder of their life. Their guidance would rather destroy the future of their children because no way can astrology exist for a long time in this present scientific world.

STEPS REQUIRED FOR ERADICATING ASTROLOGY

Enough is enough; it's high time that all superstitions be eradicated from our society now. They are parasites and are affecting our life badly. One can often find many instances where people have wasted a lot of money and time running after astrologers with the hope of a better future. Instead of them getting a better future, it's the astrologers whose future is getting better.

Many a time, astrologers declare that future is good and you become relaxed and lazy which on the other hand makes your future bad. And when astrologers declare that future is bad, you remain mentally disturbed. Many a time, people remain un-married or get married late just because the horoscopes don't match with prospective spouse. Interestingly, one astrologer declares that horoscopes match while another one comes up with a different formula and announces that horoscopes don't match. Many a time, people start a business as advised by the astrologers when practically that business shouldn't be suiting them. Result!? They fail after sometime.

Surveys all over the world prove that the people who are into - astrology, psychic phenomena, sorcery, etc. - remain more un-happy and disturbed than those who refrain from such practices. When the sufferings come, the superstitious people wonder as to why they are suffering when they had taken every possible precaution to avoid sufferings. They rush to their saviors (fortune-tellers) who in turn give them one more explanation and suggest performing some new ritual .... and the process continues.

But, all this non-sense has to end now. Let's consider the steps required for eradicating this superstition:

Step No. 1 :

This is truly the most important and most effective step required to be taken. The government should form a committee to test the validity of astrology. The so-called prominent astrologers should be invited and asked to make readings of the past events that occured in the lives of some Test Subjects from their horoscopes. After detailed systematic testing, the committee will come to know the 'truth'. Thereafter, the government should organize and promote awareness programs about the uselessness of astrology. And then government should close down the shops of 'fortune-tellers' and all such charlatans.

Step No. 2 :

In case the government doesn't take any action in this matter, it becomes duty of the intellectuals and powerful popular personalities to take initiative and help eradicate misleading superstitions. Especially the retired ones as they have plenty of time in hand. Instead of just passing their time and waiting for the 'final call', they should do something for the betterment of society. They can form Societies, NGOs, etc. and hire some 'young legs' to eradicate such misleading superstitions.

Step No. 3 :

If the heads of T.V. and Press media test the validity of astrology and are willing to eradicate this misleading superstition, they can be of greatest help.

Step No. 4 :

If acclaimed authors research the validity of fortune-telling systems and write books about their futility, it can be very helpful.

Step No. 5 :

In today's 'Mobile Age', we can get all types of knowledge sitting in the comfort of our homes. I know that living in imaginary worlds provides great pleasure but it can also yield 'drastic' consequences at times. You must also make efforts to know the 'Truth' for your own benefit... if not others'!!!

EFFORTS MADE BY THE AUTHOR

Besides losing more than five hundred thousand rupees (approx. $10000) and devoting three years in research and writing, I myself have made the following efforts:

Effort No. 1 :

Many advertisements were given in local newspapers like "Award Rs.1,00,000 offered for the astrologer who would prove that astrology works" from February 2008 to May 2009. But only three astrologers showed up and they, too, left without taking the test. Later, award money was raised to Rs. 10 lakh but still nobody seems willing to claim the award - maybe Rs. 10 lakh is a very small amount!!!

Effort No. 2 :

I sent copies of the manuscript to 17 celebrity test subjects whose horoscopes have been interpreted in this book. Apart from them, about 100 copies were sent to other national and international celebrities, requesting their initiative in this matter.

Effort No. 3 :

I sent the detail of my research-work to the heads of prominent national media in India. I called and even personally met some of them in Delhi requesting their initiative in this matter.

Effort No. 4 :

In February 2008, I personally delivered the copies of my manuscript to the offices of - Mrs. Pratibha Devi Singh Patil (President of India), Dr. Manmohan Singh (Prime Minister of India), Mrs. Sonia Gandhi (President, Indian National Congress), Mr. Arjun Singh (Human Resource Development Minister), Mr. P. R. Das Munshi (Information and Broadcasting Minister) and Dr. Karan Singh (Member of Rajya

Sabha and former prince of pre-independence State of Jammu and Kashmir).

Effort No. 5 :

So, well, till date... I haven't received any response from the people who could have been of great help in this cause and now I don't even expect anything from them. So, I am now considering legal action against the astrologers and all those who promote them.

THE FINAL CHALLENGE
AWARD Rs. 10,00,000

Well, let's come to the point now:

If you are a fortune-teller, I am sure that you are offended by this book. Well, here's your golden chance to prove me wrong. I have a very simple contest for you. By winning this contest, you will not only prove that astrology works but also win an award of one million Indian rupees. This will be your highest service to astrology. Soon, you will become a household name and within no time... a billionaire!!!

In case, you are not an astrologer but still a firm believer in astrology, kindly ask your astrologer to prove me wrong.

So, what are you waiting for, dear Sir/Madam? Contact me as soon as possible.

Rakesh Anand

Author: Astrology Tested FAKE
(Hindi Version: Jyotish JHOOTH Sabit Hua)

WWW.CITYOFHUMANS.INFO